God's Perfect Plan

Exploring Bible Prophecy from Genesis to Revelation

By Marni Shideler McKenzie

Book 2 - Lessons 11-20

Explorer's Bible Study
2652 Hwy. 46 South
P.O. Box 425
Dickson, TN 37056-0425
1-615-446-7316
www.explorerbiblestudy.org

Reprinted 2007

ISBN: 978-1-889015-69-9

Cover Design and Original Artwork by Troy D. Russell

We believe the Bible is God's Word, a divine revelation, in the original language verbally inspired
in its entirety, and that it is the supreme infallible authority in all matters of faith and conduct.
(2 Peter 1:21; 2 Timothy 3:16)

Printed in the United States of America

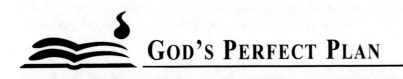

GOD'S PERFECT PLAN   LESSON 11

Daily Bible Study Questions

Study Procedure: Read the Scripture references before answering questions. Unless otherwise instructed, use the Bible only in answering questions. Some questions may be more difficult than others but try to answer as many as you can. Pray for God's wisdom and understanding as you study and don't be discouraged if some answers are not obvious at first.

FIRST DAY: Review of Lesson 10

1. What was most meaningful to you in the notes from last week?

2. List the names of the four world powers of Daniel 7.

3. Name as many characteristics as you can remember about the *"little horn"* that emerged from among the ten horns of the fourth beast.

4. What person from history prefigured the end-time Antichrist?

5. Comment on one or two things that you have learned so far in this study of prophecy that have increased your faith or made you reevaluate your present actions or choices.

SECOND DAY: Read Daniel 9:1-23

6. What had Daniel been reading that caused him to begin this particular prayer for his nation?

    Scriptures, according to the word of the Lord given to ~~Jeremiah~~ Jeremiah the prophet.

7. After beginning with a statement of praise in verse 4, with what did Daniel continue?

    Plea to God to ~~to~~ forgive Israel of their sins and take away the curses + judgement on them.

Page 1

8. What did Daniel's continual use of *"us"* and *"our"* mean to you?

He is praying for Israel as a nation.

9. (a) What did Daniel request of God in verses 15-19?

Turn away God's anger + wrath on Israel.

(b) On what grounds did he dare to ask this?

That he was a servant of God

10. Write the phrase(s) that described how soon God responded to Daniel's prayer by sending Gabriel to help him understand the vision.

20 While I was speaking + praying, confessing my sin + my people's sin + making my requests to the Lord Gabriel came

THIRD DAY: Read Daniel 9:24-27

11. In Daniel 9:24, seventy weeks were determined by God to do some specific things in the *"holy city."* What things were determined? (**Note:** *"Seventy weeks"* was the Hebrew way of saying "seventy sevens" or for the modern reader, 70 x 7 = 490. Most Bible scholars believe these weeks to refer to years, not days, weeks, or months.)

Finish transgression, to put an end to sin, to atone for wickedness, to bring in everlasting righteousness, to seal up vision + prophesy and to annoint the most holy.

12. The 490 years were to be divided into three time periods.
    (a) What was to happen in *"seven weeks"* (7 x 7 = 49 years)?

(b) What then would happen after *"sixty-two weeks"* (62 x 7 = 434 years)?

(c) What would happen in the final *"week"* (7 years)?

13. The last *"week"* or last seven years of Daniel's prophecy is described elsewhere in Scripture. Read the following Scripture references and underline the similar descriptions of that last *"week."*

    (a) (Daniel 12:1) *"At that time Michael shall stand up, the great prince who stands watch over the sons of your people; and there shall be a time of trouble, such as never was since there was a nation, even to that time. And at that time your people shall be delivered, every one who is found written in the book."*

    (b) (Revelation 3:10) *"Because you have kept My command to persevere, I also will keep you from the hour of trial which shall come upon the whole world, to test those who dwell on the earth."*

    (c) (Revelation 7:13,14) *Then one of the elders answered, saying to me, "Who are these arrayed in white robes, and where did they come from?" And I said to him, "Sir, you know." So he said to me, "These are the ones who come out of the great tribulation, and washed their robes and made them white in the blood of the Lamb."*

    (d) (Jeremiah 30:7) *"Alas! For that day is great, so that none is like it; and it is the time of Jacob's trouble, but he shall be saved out of it."*

    (e) (Matthew 24:15-22) *"Therefore when you see the 'abomination of desolation,' spoken of by Daniel the prophet, standing in the holy place"* (whoever reads, let him understand), *"then let those who are in Judea flee to the mountains. Let him who is on the housetop not go down to take anything out of his house. And let him who is in the field not go back to get his clothes. But woe to those who are pregnant and to those who are nursing babies in those days! And pray that your flight may not be in winter or on the Sabbath. For then there will be great tribulation, such as has not been since the beginning of the world until this time, no, nor ever shall be. And unless those days were shortened, no flesh would be saved; but for the elect's sake those days will be shortened."*

14. Given the date for restoring Jerusalem's wall and moat as 445 BC (by command of Artaxerxes), try to do the math to find the year that Messiah would be cut off. (**Note:** A Jewish month was 30 days and a year was 360 days. So, Jewish years have to be recalculated in our time of 365-day years. Remember when calculating, that years go from larger to smaller in "Before Christ" or BC dating. Also, there is not a "zero" year between 1 BC and AD 1.)

    (a) 49 + 434 = 483 Hebrew years x 360 days = _____ days.

    (b) _____ divided by 365 days = _____ years (our time).
          answer from (a)

    (c) _____ years - 445 BC = _____ + 1 = AD_____.
          answer from (b)

15. If *"Messiah the Prince"* is Jesus, then...

    (a) who is *"the prince who is to come"* who makes a covenant for the last seven years of this prophecy but breaks it in the middle? (See Revelation 13:1-8.)

(b) What will he do on or after the *"middle of the week"*?

(c) Find and write down the New Testament reference to the *"abomination of desolation"* mentioned in Daniel 9:27. You may use a concordance if it is not listed in your Bible column references.

FOURTH DAY: Read Daniel 11

Note: Daniel 11:1-35 has already been fulfilled exactly as God foretold in these verses by the actions of the rulers from Persia and Greece who came to power after Daniel's day. That being so, consideration here will only be given to the verses seen by many scholars as not yet having been fulfilled—interesting for our study because they add more to the description of the coming evil ruler called the Antichrist.

16. List several facts about or characteristics of the king described in Daniel 11:36-39.

17. Who from the earlier lessons on Daniel's prophecies does this man resemble? (Give references.)

18. When *"at the time of the end"* (verse 40) the king of the South (Egypt) and the king of the North (Syria) come like a whirlwind to attack the evil king, who is prophesied to win?

19. List the other nations mentioned in verses 41-43 with a short explanation beside each as to what happens to them.

20. What will divert his attention?

21. What will finally happen to him?

FIFTH DAY: Read Daniel 12

22. To when does *"at that time"* in Daniel 12:1 refer?

23. What is predicted for Israel in these opening verses?

24. In Daniel 12:4 what interesting phrase was given to describe *"the time of the end"* when these prophecies would be applied? Comment, if you can, on this.

25. Daniel was very concerned about how long his people would have to endure *"a time of trouble, such as there never was since there was a nation."*
    (a) What did he hear from the two speaking to one another across the riverbank about the length of that time period?

    (b) Daniel was not given complete details of the end, but he was told that 1290 days would remain after the *"daily sacrifice is taken away, and the abomination of desolation is set up."* Find and write down the verse from an earlier passage in Daniel that mentioned these activities.

    (c) What person was responsible for these actions according to Daniel 9:26?

26. Daniel is told to rest and is promised what in verse 13?

TROUBLE FOR ISRAEL

Daniel's Prayer (Daniel 9:1-19)

In the excitement of studying Bible prophecy, there is a danger that the student might forget one of the necessary daily disciplines of the Christian life—prayer. Whether because of a desperate need for understanding about a problem of national importance, as in Daniel's case, or because of overflowing gratitude for a life that is at the moment peaceful, God's children should regularly stop for meaningful communication with Him. In this chapter, the vital components of prayer were present: praise, **penitence**, and **petition**. Each will be examined.

The motivation for this particular prayer-time in Daniel's life was a passage he had read from the prophecies of Jeremiah. Jeremiah was the prophet whom God gave to Judah for forty years to warn them of the certain judgment facing them and how best to get through it. The nation of Judah as a whole failed to obey Jeremiah's words from God, but Daniel took the words seriously and went to God with what he had just learned from Jeremiah's scrolls. The following verses were probably the cause of Daniel's going into serious prayer and fasting at this time:

And this whole land shall be a desolation and an astonishment, and these nations shall serve the king of Babylon seventy years (Jeremiah 25:11).

Thus says the LORD of hosts, the God of Israel, to all who were carried away captive, whom I have caused to be carried away from Jerusalem to Babylon: Build houses and dwell in them; plant gardens and eat their fruit. Take wives and beget sons and daughters; and take wives for your sons and give your daughters to husbands, so that they may bear sons and daughters; that you may be increased there, and not diminished. And seek the peace of the city where I have caused you to be carried away captive, and pray to the LORD for it; for in its peace you will have peace. For thus says the LORD of hosts, the God of Israel: Do

not let your prophets and your diviners who are in your midst deceive you, nor listen to your dreams which you cause to be dreamed. For they prophesy falsely to you in My name; I have not sent them, says the LORD. For thus says the LORD: After seventy years are completed at Babylon, I will visit you and perform My good word toward you, and cause you to return to this place (Jeremiah 29:4-10).

Doing the Math

Daniel knew the year—605 BC in the modern method of stating dates—that he had been taken captive in the first wave of Babylon's conquest of Judah. Daniel 9:1 set the date for this prayer at the first year of Darius' rule over the Chaldeans, which historians have set at 538 BC According to Daniel's own calculations, then, the seventy years were almost up. He wanted Jeremiah's prophecy to come true, but the earlier visions he had received personally, years before, seemed to indicate that Israel faced still more hard times. So, Daniel did the right thing; he entered into serious prayer to ask God to let the judgment be over for Israel and to let them return to their land as Jeremiah had prophesied.

Praise (Daniel 9:4)

As Jesus taught His disciples in the New Testament, praise comes first when communicating with God. Whether alone or in a group, approach to God should begin with the focus on Him and not on self. Besides individual expressions praising His perfect character, music and Scripture can also be used when approaching Him. Through praise, He receives His rightful recognition from us, while we are reminded again that nothing we can ever need is out of the realm of His great power and love. When we pause to consider just how great He is, our faith is built up to believe that He is able and willing to answer our prayers. Praise brings the proper perspective to our problems.

Penitence (Daniel 9:5-15)

The second element of effective prayer is penitence, an honest expression of remorse or sorrow over our sins, *"If we confess our sins, He is faithful and just to forgive us our sins and to cleanse us from all unrighteousness"* (1 John 1:9). "To confess" in Greek is *homologeo* and means "to speak the same thing." That means that in prayer we take time to admit to God what we have done by calling it the same thing He calls it—sin. It is an essential part of receiving forgiveness. It really is only logical because how can a person be forgiven for something he is not willing to admit he has done? So, following praise, should be a time of penitence before the Lord.

Daniel's confession of sin was interesting because he identified himself with the sins of his nation by frequently using *"us," "we,"* and *"our,"* even though the Biblical record of his life revealed no such personal sin. Such identification was an appropriate action, because as a Jew he was a part of whatever his nation had done, just like, though we may not approve, we are a part of whatever our nation has done. Daniel was specific in listing the sins of Israel as a persistent disobedience to the clearly stated laws of Scripture and the continual warnings of the prophets. Daniel also stated that God was absolutely righteous in bringing judgment upon them.

Petition (Daniel 9:16-19)

Not because they deserved it, but because God's own name and reputation were being damaged by association with them, Daniel begged God to end the judgment of captivity on Israel. Daniel stated that his only hope for forgiveness and relief for the nation was not *"because of our righteous deeds, but because of Your great mercies"* (Daniel 9:18). With great passion, Daniel ended his prayer with this petition: *"O Lord, hear! O Lord, forgive! O Lord, listen and act! Do not delay for Your own sake, my God, for Your city and Your people are called by Your name"* (Daniel 9:19).

Gabriel, God's Messenger (Daniel 9:20-23)

While Daniel was still praying, in fact, when he first began to pray (Daniel 9:23), God **dispatched** Gabriel, His messenger angel, to appear to Daniel again. Gabriel was sent to give Daniel

"skill to understand" both what he had read in Jeremiah and what he had seen in a previous vision (Daniel 9:23). This is a wonderful example of the effectiveness of serious prayer. God heard and responded. He still wants to direct the lives of His children today with truthful information which only He can provide. So, when confused, pray.

The Seventy-Weeks Prophecy (Daniel 9:20-27)

Daniel had read Jeremiah's prophecy which stated that seventy years would be the extent of Babylon's power over Judah. Here, using the seventy in a different way, God revealed that He had a future plan for His people beyond allowing them to return to their land as promised. He would allow that return, but He would also use an historic command concerning that return to set the prophetic clock ticking for other matters related to Israel's future.

As explained briefly in the questions on this passage, the word *"weeks"* in the Hebrew meant "sevens." So, while seventy years of captivity were about to end, verse 24 stated that seventy sevens *"are determined for your people and for your holy city"* to end all sin and the punishment that follows it as well as finally bringing the nation into a relationship of *"everlasting righteousness"* which would fulfill all the prophecies and establish permanently the Most Holy Place in God's temple (Daniel 9:24). From the text, as well as what can be learned from Revelation, the seventy sevens described years. So, 490 years were left to specifically bring to pass all the prophecies pertaining to Israel. However, the 490 years would not run **consecutively**, but would be divided into three phases.

Phase One

Phase One would begin when a command was given to restore and build Jerusalem including her street and wall, which, literally, in Hebrew, were her open square and moat. There were at least four different commands issued concerning the rebuilding of Jerusalem by first Cyrus, then Darius, and finally Artaxerxes, all who were rulers of Medo-Persia. However, only one of them included the rebuilding of the wall of Jerusalem which was necessary before a moat or open square could be defined and constructed. This command was issued by King Aratxerxes in 445 BC. The prophecy stated that from the time that that command was issued until the Messiah would be revealed to Israel was a period of seven "sevens" or 49 years and then sixty-two "sevens" or 434 years. Bible historians believe the 49 years covered the repair and reconstruction of Jerusalem which ended with the covenant renewal celebration in Jerusalem in 396 BC.

Phase Two

It should be noted that a Hebrew year was 360 days long, and a Hebrew month was 30 days. Following the 49 years for the rebuilding of Jerusalem, including wall and street, was to be a period of 62 more *"weeks"* or 434 years before the Messiah appeared (Daniel 9:25). In the late 1800's, a Bible scholar named Sir Robert Anderson calculated with these figures that the coming of Messiah would be in AD 32, even noting the date as April 6! Some scholars differ a year or two from this figure, but even the "untrained" mathematician can calculate the time of the death of Messiah fairly accurately. Regardless of the year in our calendar, Jesus fulfilled Zechariah 9:9 on the exact day that God had ordained by entering Jerusalem on a donkey to be identified as Israel's long-awaited King Messiah. A few days later His crucifixion on Passover fulfilled Daniel 9:26: *"And after the sixty-two weeks Messiah shall be cut off, but not for Himself...."* The death of Messiah would be followed by the destruction of Jerusalem and the temple by the *"people of the prince who is to come."* From history, we know that the Romans destroyed Jerusalem and the temple in AD 70, so a clue is given here that the *"prince who is to come"* would be associated with that Roman empire.

Phase Three

The last *"week"* or seven years that remained in the seventy sevens of God's dealing with Israel appears to be yet in the future. The gap between the 69 weeks already fulfilled (7 sevens and 62 sevens) and the final week of years can be termed the *"times of the Gentiles"* when God's program for all non-Jewish nations is carried out. Israel disappeared as a

nation for nineteen centuries as the Gentile nations rose and fell without having to consider her, and only in 1948 did she emerge as a recognizable national entity. The final seven years of Israel's— as well as the world's—existence on this present earth were outlined briefly in Daniel 9:27. A world leader out of the old Roman empire will rise; he is called here *"the prince who is to come."* He will make a covenant or treaty with Israel for a seven-year period, but he will break it at the mid-point—after 3 ½ years—by stopping the sacrifices and offerings in the apparently rebuilt temple in Jerusalem and committing the worst **abomination** there in history which will bring about its complete **desolation**. The word *"wing"* in the passage is a **superlative** meaning in this particular context, the worst possible abomination.

More Information for Daniel (Daniel 10-11)

In Daniel 10, Daniel had been fasting and praying for three weeks when he received an overwhelming vision of a glorious and powerful man. He was given some information about the spiritual warfare that had been occurring unseen by earthly eyes. In Daniel 11:1-35 many details were given about battles involving three future rulers of Persia, a *"mighty king"* from Greece (Alexander the Great), the king of the North, commonly believed to be from Syria, and the king of the South, or of Egypt. Historians are shocked at how perfectly these complicated prophecies were fulfilled in the years following. However, for the purpose of this study, the Scripture beginning with Daniel 11:36 will be examined, since it seems to give more information about that *"prince who is to come."*

Antiochus and the Antichrist

As described in the previous lesson, a very wicked ruler from the Seleucid dynasty of Greece, named Antiochus IV, or Ephiphanes, was responsible for terrible destruction in Israel (Daniel 11:30,31). The *"abomination of desolation"* accomplished by him was the sacrificing of pigs on the holy altar and the erection of the altar of the pagan god Zeus over the altar of burnt offerings in the Jewish temple. Antiochus Epiphanes is viewed by many to be a "type" or foreshadowing of the future Antichrist. The prefix "anti" in Latin can mean "instead of" or "against." The Antichrist is a man who will try to take the place of Christ in the eyes of an unprepared world before Christ's return to earth in great power. These characteristics of Antichrist seem to be prophesied in Daniel 11:36:

1. Self-willed: This "king" will not serve under another for very long. He will insist on his own will.

2. Ambitious, full of pride: Humility will be absent from this ruler's character as he insists on his own superiority to any other god or even the true God, against Whom he will speak blasphemies.

3. Self-sufficient: He will show no regard for the *"God of his fathers nor the desire of women"* (Daniel 11:37).

4. Power-hungry: The only god he will recognize or honor is the "god" of power. With much wealth he will pursue this (Daniel 11:38).

5. Unafraid: Without hesitation, he will attack the *"strongest fortresses with a foreign god"* causing changes in leadership and division of land (Daniel 11:39).

The Wicked King's Battle Plan (Daniel 11:40-45)

"At the time of the end"—most likely referring to the last seven years of chapter nine of Daniel's prophetic outline—the Antichrist will be attacked by Syria (North) and Egypt (South). He will win that confrontation and then enter the Glorious Land, Israel. The surrounding nations Edom, Moab, and Ammon will escape him at that time, but Egypt will not. The wealth of Egypt will become his while Libya and Ethiopia *"follow at his heels,"* apparently ready to do whatever he commands. When news of the *"east and the north"* trouble him, he will leave to fight there. Many scholars believe that this may be where the Gog and Magog battle described in Ezekiel 38 and 39 fits into the seven last years, when the Antichrist publicly reveals his desire for world-dominance and demonstrates his great power by conquering Russia, Persia (Iran), Gomer

(Germany), Togarmah (Turkey), Ethiopia, and Libya as they unite to fight Israel when she was enjoying a sense of peace because of the covenant of protection with the Antichrist. Following that victory, Antichrist will set up *"the tents of his palace between the seas and the glorious holy mountain"* to establish his claim of control of Israel, in direct violation of his covenant to protect them. However, the prophecy warns *"yet he shall come to his end, and no one will help him"* (Daniel 11:45).

Trouble Like Never Before (Daniel 12:1-13)

At the time that the evil king or Antichrist breaks covenant with Israel, Michael, the warrior angel who watches over Israel, will ready himself for battle in the spiritual realm. A devastating time of trouble will face Israel on earth as well, but those who love God, whose names are *"written in the book"* will be delivered. Those already dead will wake, some to *"everlasting life"* and others to *"everlasting contempt."* Resurrection here is promised to everyone, but the place in which each spends eternity will be decided by his or her relationship with God. Even though he was probably eager to hear more, Daniel was told to *"shut up the words, and seal the book until the time of the end"* when *"many shall run to and fro, and knowledge shall increase"* (Daniel 12:4). Does that not describe our present time? The invention of the microchip or microprocessor which allowed the miniaturization of computers and their placement in so many things has caused information to be shared worldwide and at amazing speeds. In addition, the frequency and ease of travel afforded to modern man, makes it appear that now is the time for Daniel's prophecies to come true.

Daniel heard a few more important facts which he recorded faithfully. In Daniel 12:7 he heard that the time of the terrible trouble for Israel will last three and a half years (*"time, times, and half a time"*). Daniel asked one more question when he did not understand: *"My lord, what shall be the end of these things?"* Reminded that all these things were for much later, and that good and evil would continue to conflict for a long time to come, Daniel was given a bit more information: from the time that the Antichrist breaks his covenant with Israel, stopping her temple sacrifices and setting up the *"abomination of desolation"* which declares him to be God, there will be 1,290 days, or 3 years and 7 months. The last warning was for those remaining who trust in God: they should wait patiently forty-five days longer. The meaning of these two additions of one month and then another month and a half to the 3 ½ years or 1,260 days used elsewhere as the time-frame of the last days has not been **conclusively** explained. The instruction to wait patiently, however, can be understood. Like Daniel, ours is not to worry, but to rest in God's protection. After all, we Christians share the same promise of resurrection to life eternal as Daniel, no matter what happens on this earth.

VOCABULARY

1. **abomination:** something disgusting, unlawful, detestable, or loathsome
2. **conclusively:** in a form which puts to an end any questions or doubts
3. **consecutively:** following in uninterrupted succession
4. **desolation:** having been laid to waste; devastation
5. **dispatched:** set off to a particular destination or on specific business
6. **penitence:** an expression or feeling of remorse for one's sins or misdeeds
7. **petition:** a solemn request by prayer
8. **superlative:** a term of comparison that shows the extreme extent or level of something

Notes

Notes

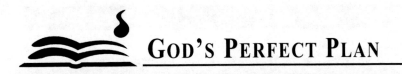

Daily Bible Study Questions

Study Procedure: Read the Scripture references before answering questions. Unless otherwise instructed, use the Bible only in answering questions. Some questions may be more difficult than others but try to answer as many as you can. Pray for God's wisdom and understanding as you study and don't be discouraged if some answers are not obvious at first.

FIRST DAY: Review of Lesson 11

   1. Describe the three important components of Daniel's prayer?

   2. After reading Jeremiah's prophecy about the seventy years of captivity, about what was Daniel concerned?

   3. What did you learn that might encourage you to be more faithful in your praying to God?

   4. Summarize what Daniel was told would occur during the 490 years set apart to complete God's promises to Israel. (You may refer to the notes on Daniel 9, 11, and 12.)

SECOND DAY:

   5. The *"time of trouble"* for Israel will be stopped and all remaining prophetical promises to the nation of Israel will be fulfilled when Messiah returns to earth. There are actually more Bible references to the coming of Christ to earth in power as "Conquering King" than there are to His first appearance in humility as "Suffering Savior." Read some examples of these prophecies in the following passages and summarize at least one thing you learn from each one about what will happen when Christ returns to earth.

(a) (Psalm 2:6-9) *"Yet I have set My King on My holy hill of Zion. I will declare the decree: The LORD has said to Me, 'You are My Son, today I have begotten You. Ask of Me, and I will give You the nations for Your inheritance, and the ends of the earth for Your possession. You shall break them with a rod of iron; You shall dash them to pieces like a potter's vessel.'"*

(b) (Isaiah 9:6,7) *"For unto us a Child is born, unto us a Son is given; and the government will be upon His shoulder. And His name will be called Wonderful, Counselor, Mighty God, Everlasting Father, Prince of Peace. Of the increase of His government and peace there will be no end, upon the throne of David and over His kingdom, to order it and establish it with judgment and justice from that time forward, even forever. The zeal of the LORD of hosts will perform this."*

(c) (Isaiah 11:3-5) *"His delight is in the fear of the LORD, and He shall not judge by the sight of His eyes, nor decide by the hearing of His ears; but with righteousness He shall judge the poor, and decide with equity for the meek of the earth; He shall strike the earth with the rod of His mouth, and with the breath of His lips He shall slay the wicked. Righteousness shall be the belt of His loins, and faithfulness the belt of His waist."*

(d) (Isaiah 26:20,21) *"Come, my people, enter your chambers, and shut your doors behind you; hide yourself, as it were, for a little moment, until the indignation is past. For behold, the LORD comes out of His place to punish the inhabitants of the earth for their iniquity; the earth will also disclose her blood, and will no more cover her slain."*

(e) (Jeremiah 23:5,6) *"Behold, the days are coming,"* says the LORD, *"that I will raise to David a Branch of righteousness; a King shall reign and prosper, and execute judgment and righteousness in the earth. In His days Judah will be saved, and Israel will dwell safely; now this is His name by which He will be called: THE LORD OUR RIGHTEOUSNESS."*

(f) (Daniel 2:44) *"And in the days of these kings the God of heaven will set up a kingdom which shall never be destroyed; and the kingdom shall not be left to other people; it shall break in pieces and consume all these kingdoms, and it shall stand forever."*

(g) (Daniel 7:13,14) *"I was watching in the night visions, and behold, One like the Son of Man, coming with the clouds of heaven! He came to the Ancient of Days, and they brought Him near before Him. Then to Him was given dominion and glory and a kingdom, that all peoples, nations, and languages should serve Him. His dominion is an everlasting dominion, which shall not pass away, and His kingdom the one which shall not be destroyed."*

(h) (Zechariah 14:1-9) *"Behold, the day of the LORD is coming, and your spoil will be divided in your midst. For I will gather all the nations to battle against Jerusalem; the city shall be taken, the houses rifled, and the women ravished. Half of the city shall go into captivity, but the remnant of the people shall not be cut off from the city. Then the LORD will go forth and fight against those nations, as He fights in the day of battle. And in that day His feet will stand on the Mount of Olives, which faces Jerusalem on the east. And the Mount of Olives shall be split in two, from east to west, making a very large valley; half of the mountain shall move toward the north and half of it toward the south. Then you shall flee through My mountain valley, for the mountain valley shall reach to Azal. Yes, you shall flee as you fled from the earthquake in the days of Uzziah king of Judah. Thus the LORD my God will come, and all the saints with You. It shall come to pass in that day that there will be no light; the lights will diminish. It shall be one day which is known to the LORD—neither day nor night. But at evening time it shall happen that it will be light. And in that day it shall be that living waters shall flow from Jerusalem, half of them toward the eastern sea and half of them toward the western sea; in both summer and winter it shall occur. And the LORD shall be King over all the earth. In that day it shall be—'The LORD is one, and His name one.'"*

THIRD DAY:

6. Read these prophecies from the New Testament and then match them with the best summary of the facts associated with the return of Christ.

_____ (a) (Matthew 24:27-30) *"For as the lightning comes from the east and flashes to the west, so also will the coming of the Son of Man be. For wherever the carcass is, there the eagles will be gathered together. Immediately after the tribulation of those days the sun will be darkened, and the moon will not give its light; the stars will fall from heaven, and the powers of the heavens will be shaken. Then the sign of the Son of Man will appear in heaven, and then all the tribes of the earth will mourn, and they will see the Son of Man coming on the clouds of heaven with power and great glory."*

_____ (b) (Matthew 24:37-39) *"But as the days of Noah were, so also will the coming of the Son of Man be. For as in the days before the flood, they were eating and drinking, marrying and giving in marriage, until the day that Noah entered the ark, and did not know until the flood came and took them all away, so also will the coming of the Son of Man be."*

_____ (c) (Acts 1:11) *...who also said, "Men of Galilee, why do you stand gazing up into heaven? This same Jesus, who was taken up from you into heaven, will so come in like manner as you saw Him go into heaven."*

_____ (d) (Jude 1:14,15) *Now Enoch, the seventh from Adam, prophesied about these men also, saying, "Behold, the Lord comes with ten thousands of His saints, to execute judgment on all, to convict all who are ungodly among them of all their ungodly deeds which they have committed in an ungodly way, and of all the harsh things which ungodly sinners have spoken against Him."*

_____ (e) (Revelation 1:7) *"Behold, He is coming with clouds, and every eye will see Him, even they who pierced Him. And all the tribes of the earth will mourn because of Him. Even so, Amen."*

_____ (f) (Revelation 19:11-16) *"Now I saw heaven opened, and behold, a white horse. And He who sat on him was called Faithful and True, and in righteousness He judges and makes war. His eyes were like a flame of fire, and on His head were many crowns. He had a name written that no one knew except Himself. He was clothed with a robe dipped in blood, and His name is called The Word of God. And the armies in heaven, clothed in fine linen, white and clean, followed Him on white horses. Now out of His mouth goes a sharp sword, that with it He should strike the nations. And He Himself will rule them with a rod of iron. He Himself treads the winepress of the fierceness and wrath of Almighty God. And He has on His robe and on His thigh a name written: KING OF KINGS AND LORD OF LORDS."*

1. Jesus will return physically and visibly from the clouds of heaven to the earth. Everyone will recognize Him.

2. The Lord, accompanied by His saints, will come to judge all ungodliness. Enoch, just seven generations after Adam, knew this and prophesied this to those living at that time.

3. The return of Jesus as King of Kings will be dramatic and spectacular. He will come on a white horse with the armies of heaven to finish the wrath of God and rule with a rod of iron.

4. Following a supernatural period of frightening darkness, Jesus will return in a great lightning flash, in the clouds, and with great glory.

5. In the same way that the eyewitnesses saw Jesus ascend to heaven in the clouds after His resurrection, eyewitnesses will also see Him return from heaven to earth.

6. Unfortunately, the world will be busily occupied with the normal routine of living and be unaware of and unprepared for His sudden return to judge them.

7. **Challenge Question:** The return of Christ is mentioned at least 318 times in the New Testament. Select a book (excluding Galatians, Philemon, and 3 John) and make a note of each reference you find in it to Christ's return or to a result of His expected return.

FOURTH DAY:

8. Many Bible students see two distinct "stages" of the return of Christ, separated by a gap in time and accomplishing different things. Read the following passages and match the appropriate heading with the Scripture.

   1. His return for the saints   2. His return with the saints

   _____ (a) (John 14:3) *"And if I go and prepare a place for you, I will come again and receive you to Myself; that where I am, there you may be also."*

   _____ (b) (1 Thessalonians 3:13) *"...so that He may establish your hearts blameless in holiness before our God and Father at the coming of our Lord Jesus Christ with all His saints."*

   _____ (c) (1 Thessalonians 4:13,14) *"But I do not want you to be ignorant, brethren, concerning those who have fallen asleep, lest you sorrow as others who have no hope. For if we believe that Jesus died and rose again, even so God will bring with Him those who sleep in Jesus."*

   _____ (d) (1 Thessalonians 4:15-18) *"For this we say to you by the word of the Lord, that we who are alive and remain until the coming of the Lord will by no means precede those who are asleep. For the Lord Himself will descend from heaven with a shout, with the voice of an archangel, and with the trumpet of God. And the dead in Christ will rise first. Then we who are alive and remain shall be caught up together with them in the clouds to meet the Lord in the air. And thus we shall always be with the Lord. Therefore comfort one another with these words."*

   _____ (e) (2 Thessalonians 2:1,2) *"Now, brethren, concerning the coming of our Lord Jesus Christ and our gathering together to Him, we ask you, not to be soon shaken in mind or troubled, either by spirit or by word or by letter, as if from us, as though the day of Christ had come."*

_____ (f) (Jude 1:14,15) *Now Enoch, the seventh from Adam, prophesied about these men also, saying, "Behold, the Lord comes with ten thousands of His saints to execute judgment on all, to convict all who are ungodly among them of all their ungodly deeds which they have committed in an ungodly way, and of all the harsh things which ungodly sinners have spoken against Him."*

9. The "catching away" of the Church to meet the Lord in the air is often called the Rapture, although that word itself does not appear in Scripture. Read the following passages and describe what occurs in each. Then summarize what they have in common.

(a) Acts 8:39

(b) 2 Corinthians 12:2,4

(c) 1 Thessalonians 4:17

(d) Revelation 12:5

(e) Summary

FIFTH DAY:

10. There are differences of opinion about the timing of the "catching away" of the Church. Read the following passages and make a note of any pattern that can be identified in the saving of the godly from the wrath of God in these examples.

(a) Noah and the flood (Read Genesis 6:6-8; 7:11-14; 8:1,13-16)

(b) Lot and the destruction of Sodom and Gomorrah (Genesis 19:15-22)

(c) Children of Israel and plagues on Egypt (Exodus 8:20-24)

(d) Paul's assurances to the Thessalonians (1 Thessalonians 1:10; 5:9)

11. We have covered many big truths so far this year in preparation for our study of Revelation. Take time right now and summarize in outline form below some of the prophetic truths you have learned that have to do specifically with God's plans for the nation of Israel. You will find it helpful to scan past lessons for what was covered there.

HE IS COMING BACK!

The Messiah: King of Israel

In the previous notes on the prophecies of Daniel, it was shown how Jesus "arrived" right on schedule—to the day, but was unrecognized by the nation of Israel and crucified. From our New Testament viewpoint, unavailable to Daniel, we know that Jesus was not defeated at the Cross. He rose to live again after three days, having fulfilled all Scripture about that part of His mission and accomplishing the work that God had given Him to do. Daniel did not know about that, but he had been trusted with future details about a fierce enemy that would rise to power after Messiah's first appearance. That enemy would cause terrible trouble for the nation of Israel—far worse than they had ever experienced. Yet, Daniel was assured that, finally, his people would be delivered. In this lesson we have begun to examine what the Scriptures have to say about the return of Christ to bring such a deliverance. Actually, there are several important events to be associated with that glorious return, and this week's lesson offered our first look.

What Daniel Did Not Know

When Daniel received the 490-year timetable for the fulfillment of all the judgments and blessings prophesied for Israel, he most likely thought that when the "prophetic clock" began ticking, it would continue without interruption until the end. Neither he nor anyone else in the Old Testament had any way of knowing that God intended to use the unbelief of Israel as an opportunity to take the gospel to the Gentiles. God had planned a "gap" or "pause" in the prophetic plan for Israel so that He could build His Church. "Church" comes from the Greek word *ekklesia* and literally means "the called out ones." That is exactly what its members are: people "called out" from every race and nation because they believe the gospel message. We are in the "church-age" right now—God's divine "pause"— and He could end it any time He chooses because it is completely under God's control. Only He knows when the *"fullness of the Gentiles"* will come in and the "prophetic clock" will begin again to count down the last seven years of this present world.

Mysteries

God saved the explanation of several important truths for the New Testament writers and for us. In Scripture these are called mysteries. By definition, a mystery is a puzzle or problem—something not understood. In Bible-terms a mystery has these characteristics: (1) It has always been in the plan of God. (2) It was not revealed in the Old Testament. (3) It could not have been known or "figured out" unless God had chosen to reveal it in the New Testament. (4) When revealed and received, it provides a better understanding of the overall prophetic plan of God for His children. (See Ephesians 3:1-6; 1 Corinthians 2:7; and Romans 16:25.)

Blindness in Part (Romans 11:25-27)

The first mystery that needs to be examined in order to understand one of the things that will happen at the return of Jesus was explained by Paul in Romans 11:25-27: *"For I do not desire, brethren, that you should be ignorant of this mystery, lest you should be wise in your own opinion, that blindness in part has happened to Israel until the fullness of the Gentiles has come in. And so all Israel will be saved, as it is written: 'The Deliverer will come out of Zion, and He will turn away ungodliness from Jacob; for this is My covenant with them, when I take away their sins.'"* Paul had been defending God's treatment of Israel and assuring his readers that God's own righteousness would cause every promise to Israel yet unfulfilled to be kept. In explanation, Paul revealed this *"mystery"* to help explain why it appeared that God had broken His covenant with Israel: Since Israel as a nation had refused to accept Jesus as their Messiah at His first coming, God had allowed the ones who failed to believe to remain spiritually "blind" as a judgment on their sin. Throughout their history, since that time, part of Israel has remained blind to the truth of the Gospel. However, when God finishes His plan for offering the gift of salvation to the non-Jews and *"the fullness of the Gentiles has come in,"* He will remove the blindness from Israel so that they—specifically those alive at that time—will recognize Jesus as their true Messiah at His return and be saved.

The "Catching Away" of the Saints (1 Corinthians 15:51,52 and 1 Thessalonians 4:15-17)

The next mystery has to do with "phase one" of Christ's return: the Rapture. As noted in the question section, the word "rapture" does not occur in the Bible. That was taken from the Latin translation of the original Greek word *harpazo* which meant "caught up" or "caught away." This phenomenon was described in the Old Testament as having been experienced by Enoch (Genesis 5:24) and Elijah (2 Kings 2:11) and in the New Testament by Philip (Acts 8:39), Paul (2 Corinthians 12:1-4), Jesus (Acts 1:9), and prophesied for the Church at Christ's return. Paul explained it in 1 Corinthians 15:51,52: *"Behold, I tell you a mystery: We shall not all sleep, but we shall all be changed—in a moment, in the twinkling of an eye, at the last trumpet. For the trumpet will sound, and the dead will be raised incorruptible, and we shall be changed."* "Sleep" was a New Testament **euphemism** for "die." Paul, who had been privately taught by the Holy Spirit (Galatians 1:15-19), was God's chosen vessel for explaining many things to the world. As a special blessing and surprise, God let Paul reveal that there will be a day when Christ will return and all Christians, living and dead, will receive new, glorified, and **incorruptible** bodies. What will they be like? We can assume that they will have the same characteristics as Jesus' resurrected body: recognizable as belonging to the same person as before; unlimited by physical barriers, time, or space; but still having a physical form that can be seen, touched, and even fed (1 John 3:2). In Paul's first letter to the Thessalonians, he again described this mystery, adding a few more details. He told them that God intended for it to be a comfort to His people:

> But I do not want you to be ignorant, brethren, concerning those who have fallen asleep, lest you sorrow as others who have no hope. For if we believe that Jesus died and rose again, even so God will bring with Him those who sleep in Jesus. For this we say to you by the word of the Lord, that we who are alive and remain until the coming of the Lord will by no means precede those who are asleep. For the Lord Himself will descend from heaven with a shout, with the voice of an archangel, and with the trumpet of God. And the dead in Christ will rise first. Then we who are alive and remain shall be caught up together with them in the clouds to meet the Lord in the air. And thus we shall always be with the Lord. Therefore comfort one another with these words (1 Thessalonians 4:13-18).

Timing Debated

There is a great deal of debate among very sincere Christians as to just when this "catching away" will occur in relation to the last *"week"* or seven years of Daniel's prophecy. Because of several verses that promise help in and through trouble or danger, some believe that the Rapture will occur at the 3 ½ year point, after the sixth "seal" judgment. Others believe that the Church will not be *"caught up"* to meet Christ until the end of the seven year tribulation period. A biblical example of this would be the Children of Israel during the plagues in Egypt. They were not removed from Egypt, but endured some of the plagues, were spared from others, but were protected throughout and ultimately delivered by God's power. However, the outline given in Revelation (to be discussed later) as well as the examples of God's treatment of Noah and Lot, lend support to those who believe the Lord will return for His saints before the trouble or tribulation begins. In addition, several of Jesus' parables and the customs for Jewish weddings so often included in His teachings emphasized a surprising suddenness to His appearance. Furthermore, because no sign is given to be watched for before that event, while several are given before Christ will return to the earth to finish off the enemies of God, there seems to be much in favor of the saints meeting the Lord in the air before the tribulation period, going to heaven with Him, and then returning with Him at the final moment of victory, from heaven and to the earth. Nevertheless, the timing of the "catching away" should not be allowed to cause contention among well-meaning Bible students. The promise of meeting the Lord in the air, exchanging old bodies for new glorious ones, and never again being separated from Him or our Christian loved ones is worth waiting for whenever it occurs!

An Important Comment

After reading so many verses placed in the questions section describing the unmistakable return of Christ in the clouds with His saints, to defeat the enemies of Israel, to set up an eternal worldwide kingdom, and to act as righteous Judge over the guilty men and angels, it might seem unusual that some people still do not believe that Jesus will really return one day. In the first three centuries after the Ascension of Christ, it was universally taught, accepted, and expected that He would return as He promised. However, as the life of the Church began blending more with the powers of the world, some leaders began to misuse and abuse the Scriptures. So, off and on ever since, there have been many who have overlooked or neglected the literally hundreds of references to the return of Christ in power and glory.

There were (and still are) differing views among those who refused to believe He would return. Some taught that the prophecies should be taken only symbolically—as examples of the struggle of good against evil. Some taught that all the prophecies had already been fulfilled at some time in the past history of the world. Others, discouraged by the long absence of Israel as an identifiable nation, began to teach that the Church had replaced Israel in God's plan and that God was finished with Israel. In contrast, the view followed in this study is that the Scriptures should be taken at their simplest and most basic meaning, letting them mean what they say. The Bible is made up of history, poetry, proverb, parable, and prophecy. From the text and context, the meaning of each passage must be discerned. The Holy Spirit, of course, promises to help us. This return to the careful study of Scripture as the inspired and protected Word of God began several centuries ago at the time of the Reformation. Then men and women literally lost their lives while defending their belief that God meant what He had said in His Word and that that Word should be available to every person, in his own language, to be studied for himself. They refused to accept the substitute meanings, man-made customs, or church laws that attempted to replace God's clear Word with the desires of men. It is just as important in this day and age that we bravely stand to defend Scripture, being carefully trained to rightly divide the Word of truth.

The Return of Christ Involves Several Things

Introduced in this lesson was the "catching away" of the Church to meet the Lord *"in the air."* However there are several events preceding and accompanying Christ's return to the earth, and each of these will be studied in future lessons. Most will be treated fully as they are mentioned in the book of Revelation, which will be examined chapter by chapter.

VOCABULARY

1. **euphemism:** a substitution for a word or expression that is thought to be too strong, blunt, or painful for another person (example: use "to pass away" instead of "to die")
2. **incorruptible:** not subject to decay

Notes

Notes

Daily Bible Study Questions

Study Procedure: Read the Scripture references before answering questions. Unless otherwise instructed, use the Bible only in answering questions. Some questions may be more difficult than others but try to answer as many as you can. Pray for God's wisdom and understanding as you study and don't be discouraged if some answers are not obvious at first.

FIRST DAY: Review of Lesson 12

1. What are some reasons for believing that Christ will return to us some day?

    Prophesy
    Prophesey come true

2. Define a bible *"mystery."*

    Something we are told in the word of God, but don't understand.

3. Name and describe the mysteries mentioned in the notes.

4. When, in relation to the last seven years, do you think the *harpazo* or "catching away" will occur? Why?

SECOND DAY:

5. Read the following passage, which is the first in which the church is specifically mentioned, and answer the questions that follow.

    (Matthew 16:13-19) *When Jesus came into the region of Caesarea Philippi, He asked His disciples, saying, "Who do men say that I, the Son of Man, am?" So they said, "Some say John the Baptist, some Elijah, and others Jeremiah or one of the prophets." He said to them, "But who do you say that I am?" Simon Peter answered and said, "You are the Christ, the Son of the living God." Jesus answered and said to him, "Blessed are you, Simon Bar-Jonah, for flesh and blood has not revealed this to you, but My Father who is in heaven. And I also say to you that you are Peter, and on this rock I will build My church, and the gates of Hades shall not prevail against it. And I will give you the keys of the kingdom of heaven, and whatever you bind on earth will be bound in heaven, and whatever you loose on earth will be loosed in heaven."*

(a) For what did Jesus say Simon Peter was *"blessed"*?

Flesh & blood did not reveal to him that Jesus was the Christ, it was revealed to him by ~~God~~ his Father in Heaven

(b) What was the *"rock"* that would serve as the foundation for the church Jesus would build? See 1 Corinthians 3:11 and Romans 9:33. (**Note:** Peter is a translation of *petros* which means "detached stone or boulder." Rock is from the word *petra* which means "a mass of rock, a type of sure foundation" as used in Mark 15:46; Luke 6:48; and 1 Corinthians 10:4.)

Jesus ~~Peter~~, and on this rock I will build my church.

(c) What power and what authority would be given to the church which Christ would build?

Gates of Hades shall not prevail against it. Keys to the kingdom of Heaven & whatever you bind on earth will be bound in Heaven. Whatever you loose ~~and~~ on earth will be loosed in Heaven.

6. The Bible gives several descriptive "pictures" of the church. Read the following passages, and then identify the "picture" being given and summarize what you learn about the purpose or nature of the church.

   (a) 1 Corinthians 12:12-31:

   (b) Ephesians 2:17-22:

THIRD DAY:

7. By revealing some more "mysteries" to the New Testament reader, God gave important details about His relationship to the church. Read the following passages and then match them with the correct explanation or summary given below.

   _____ (a) (Colossians 1:26,27) *"...the mystery which has been hidden from ages and from generations, but now has been revealed to His saints. To them God willed to make known what are the riches of the glory of this mystery among the Gentiles: which is Christ in you, the hope of glory."*

   _____ (b) (Ephesians 3:1-6) *"For this reason I, Paul, the prisoner of Christ Jesus for you Gentiles—if indeed you have heard of the dispensation of the grace of*

God which was given to me for you, how that by revelation He made known to me the mystery (as I have briefly written already, by which, when you read, you may understand my knowledge in the mystery of Christ), which in other ages was not made known to the sons of men, as it has now been revealed by the Spirit to His holy apostles and prophets: that the Gentiles should be fellow heirs, of the same body, and partakers of His promise in Christ through the gospel...."

_____ (c) (Ephesians 6:19,20) *"...and for me, that utterance may be given to me, that I may open my mouth boldly to make known the mystery of the gospel, for which I am an ambassador in chains; that in it I may speak boldly, as I ought to speak."*

(Romans 16:25) *"Now to Him who is able to establish you according to my gospel and the preaching of Jesus Christ, according to the revelation of the mystery kept secret since the world began...."*

_____ (d) (Ephesians 5:31,32) *"For this reason a man shall leave his father and mother and be joined to his wife, and the two shall become one flesh. This is a great mystery, but I speak concerning Christ and the church."*

1. Gentiles are welcomed into the family of God through Christ as completely as the Jews!
2. Christ actually lives inside of the persons who accept Him by faith!
3. Marriage illustrates the close union Christ holds with His church.
4. The Gospel explains how the holiness of our righteous God was satisfied as His Son Jesus, perfect and sinless, offered His own blood as an atonement for all sin.

8. Summarize some of the truths you have learned so far about the nature and purpose of the church.

FOURTH DAY:

9. The New Testament makes frequent use of the description of the church as Christ's "Bride." In order to understand more fully the appropriateness of this "picture," read the following description of Jewish marriage customs adapted from several resources on Jewish culture.

The prospective groom, with the advice and approval of his father, would select a young woman to marry. Next, he and his father would meet with her and her father to consider a marriage contract or covenant. The most important part of the covenant was an agreement on the price to be paid for the bride to her father from the groom. When an agreement was reached, the couple and their fathers would seal the covenant by drinking a cup of wine. The groom would then pay the price and then leave to prepare a suitable home for his bride. She was expected to wait, always veiled when in public and accepting no attention from any other young man, until her groom returned to marry her.

The exact time of this "waiting period" was not certain. It often took a year for a young man to make suitable preparations for his bride, since it would be necessary to construct an addition to his father's house or another dwelling on his father's property. The groom's father had the final authority to say when the home was ready. So, only the groom's father knew when the wedding was likely to occur.

The bride spent her betrothal (engagement) period preparing for her groom to return. She gathered clothes and household goods and attended to whatever was necessary to make herself the most beautiful. She also selected her bridesmaids, had them waiting near her, and kept such things as lamps and oil on hand, so as to be ready at any hour for her groom's return.

When the groom's father gave permission for him to go and claim his bride, the young man and his friends gave a shout of warning to give the bride and her friends time to respond. The romantic part of this Jewish custom was the sudden "stealing" of the bride. She would wear her veil over her face until they entered the prepared wedding chamber. When the couple was in their chamber, the groom's father would call for the guests to come.

The couple would remain secluded for seven days while the wedding celebration began outside. However, the actual celebration would not begin until the couple had come together and consummated their marriage. The friend of the bridegroom would be stationed at a door so as to hear from the groom when that had occurred and relate that information to the waiting guests. The celebration would begin, but estimating just how much food and drink would last a week was not always simple! It was embarrassing but not uncommon to run short. Of course, the wealth of the groom's father would determine the quality and quantity of what was offered.

After seven days, the couple joined the public celebration for a final wedding feast. Now the bride, whose identity was hidden by a veil when she was "caught away," appeared without her face covered so that all could identify her. Following the feast, the bride and groom, now husband and wife, would begin their new life together in their prepared place.

From your knowledge of the Bible, or with the help of a concordance, find at least three Scripture passages which illustrate or allude to these customs.

Example: John the Baptist referred to the joy he had at just being the *"friend"* of the Bridegroom in John 3:28-30: *"You yourselves bear me witness, that I said, 'I am not the Christ,' but, 'I have been sent before Him.' He who has the bride is the bridegroom; but the friend of the bridegroom, who stands and hears him, rejoices greatly because of the bridegroom's voice. Therefore this joy of mine is fulfilled. He must increase, but I must decrease."*

(a)

(b)

(c)

FIFTH DAY:

10. Read the following passages and then restate the purpose or function of the church given in each.

(a) (Matthew 28:16-20) *Then the eleven disciples went away into Galilee, to the mountain which Jesus had appointed for them. When they saw Him, they worshiped Him; but some doubted. And Jesus came and spoke to them, saying, "All authority has been given to Me in heaven and on earth. Go therefore and make disciples of all the nations, baptizing them in the name of the Father and of the Son and of the Holy Spirit, teaching them to observe all things that I have commanded you; and lo, I am with you always, even to the end of the age." Amen.*

(b) (Ephesians 4:11-16) *"And He Himself gave some to be apostles, some prophets, some evangelists, and some pastors and teachers, for the equipping of the saints for the work of ministry, for the edifying of the body of Christ, till we all come to the unity of the faith and of the knowledge of the Son of God, to a perfect man, to the measure of the stature of the fullness of Christ; that we should no longer be children, tossed to and fro and carried about with every wind of doctrine, by the trickery of men, in the cunning craftiness of deceitful plotting, but, speaking the truth in love, may grow up in all things into Him who is the head—Christ—from whom the whole body, joined and knit together by what every joint supplies, according to the effective working by which every part does its share, causes growth of the body for the edifying of itself in love."*

(c) (1 Thessalonians 5:12-22) *"And we urge you, brethren, to recognize those who labor among you, and are over you in the Lord and admonish you, and to esteem them very highly in love for their work's sake. Be at peace among yourselves. Now we exhort you, brethren, warn those who are unruly, comfort the fainthearted, uphold the weak, be patient with all. See that no one renders evil for evil to anyone, but always pursue what is good both for yourselves and for all. Rejoice always, pray without ceasing, in everything give thanks; for this is the will of God in Christ Jesus for you. Do not quench the Spirit. Do not despise prophecies. Test all things; hold fast what is good. Abstain from every form of evil."*

(d) (2 Timothy 2:1,2) *"You therefore, my son, be strong in the grace that is in Christ Jesus. And the things that you have heard from me among many witnesses, commit these to faithful men who will be able to teach others also."*

(e) (Hebrews 10:25) *"...not forsaking the assembling of ourselves together, as is the manner of some, but exhorting one another, and so much the more as you see the Day approaching."*

11. From what you learned above, what area do you see as needing improvement in the church today?

GOD'S PLAN FOR THE CHURCH

Its Foundation

Jesus was the first to mention the *"church"* as a unique **entity** in response to Peter's statement of faith in Matthew 16:13-19. The concept of a church was never mentioned in the Old Testament, although like other *"mysteries"* it had been in the heart and plan of God from the beginning. There had been plenty of Old Testament Scripture assuring God's love for the Gentiles as well as His people Israel. Several famous Gentiles, like Job, Rahab, and Ruth, even came to know the true God, finding salvation in believing the promise of the coming Savior or Messiah. However, the focus of the Old Testament was on God's plans for and through Israel, especially the plan for bringing the Jewish Messiah into the world. That there would be a distinct group united in a belief in Jesus Christ as Savior of the world and that that group would be made up of both Jew and Gentile, completely equal in the sight of God, was not revealed until Jesus came. Jesus told Peter in Matthew 16, and Paul repeated in 1 Corinthians 3:11, that the foundation of that group of "called out ones" would be Jesus Himself. That church would overcome the very gates of Hell and the members of it would have spiritual power on earth to do the will and work of God. Later, Paul made clear that the Old Testament *"rock"* which would cause many to stumble, was none other than Jesus Himself: *"As it is written: 'Behold, I lay in Zion a stumbling stone and rock of offense, and whoever believes on Him will not be put to shame'"* (Romans 9:33). Further information revealing the long-hidden *"mystery"* was given in Ephesians 3:1-6 where Paul told of the revelation he had received from God *"which in other ages was not made known to the sons of men...that the Gentiles should be fellow heirs of the same body, and partakers of His promise in Christ through the gospel...."*

Two Illustrations

In the Old Testament, as in the New, salvation was through faith in Messiah. The Old Testament believers looked ahead to His coming, while New Testament believers looked back to it. However, in the Jewish mind, before God corrected this by revealing His plan for the church, a Gentile was not considered an "equal" to a Jew unless he chose also to keep the Jewish laws—in essence—becoming Jewish too. This was even an issue that had to be clarified in the early church. Look at the following illustrations to see the difference that the revealing of the *"mystery"* of the church made in seeing all men as equally accepted through faith in Christ. Truly, the requirement is faith in Jesus, not in any specific nationality or adherence to any distinct culture.

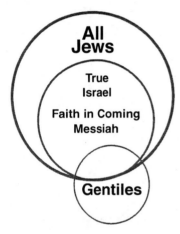

Old Testament View

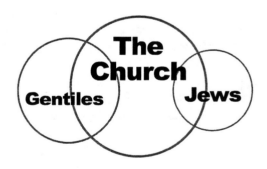

New Testament Reality

The church does not replace Israel or **nullify** God's promises to that nation. God has a definite plan for the New Testament church, just as He has a specific plan for the nation of Israel. However, for both, salvation is only through faith in Messiah.

Another Mystery Explained

While the great truths of blood sacrifice and the coming of Messiah were certainly given many times in the Old Testament, the *"mystery"* about precisely who, what, when, where, how, and why were left for the New Testament writers to explain in clear language: *"...and for me, that utterance may be given to me, that I may open my mouth boldly to make known the mystery of the gospel, for which I am an ambassador in chains; that in it I may speak boldly, as I ought to speak"* (Ephesians 6:19,20). Also: *"Now to Him who is able to establish you according to my gospel and the preaching of Jesus Christ, according to the revelation of the mystery kept secret since the world began..."* (Romans 16:25). Jesus of Nazareth was the Savior sent by God to offer His blood in atonement for all sin. Once revealed, this New Testament mystery made clear all the Old Testament prophecies. It gave a name, face, and even an address to the long-awaited Messiah. The apostle Peter said that we have been given the privilege to understand things that the prophets could not see and even the angels desired to look into (1Peter 1:12). We should never take such a privilege lightly.

Two More Mysteries

Further explanation was given to the church as to just how personal her relationship would be to her Savior and Lord:

1. Christ actually lives inside of the persons who accept Him by faith! Colossians 1:26,27: *"...the mystery which has been hidden from ages and from generations, but now has been revealed to His saints. To them God willed to make known what are the riches of the glory of this mystery among the Gentiles: which is* <u>*Christ in you, the hope of glory*</u>*"* (Emphasis added).

2. Marriage illustrates the close union Christ holds with His church! Ephesians 5:31,32: *"'For this reason a man shall leave his father and mother and be joined to his wife, and the two shall become one flesh.'* <u>*This is a great mystery, but I speak concerning Christ and the church*</u>*"* (Emphasis added). This is one of the verses that supports the idea of the church as Christ's bride.

Function of the Church

In the Scriptures examined on the Fifth Day, some of the duties of the church were given. Among the most important are (1) world **evangelism** and disciple-making (Matthew 28:16-20); (2) recognition and utilization of spiritual gifts for the careful training of the saints for the work of Christ's ministry (Ephesians 4:11-16); (3) **submission** to and appreciation for spiritual authority; (4) warning and correction of **erring** saints; (5) maintaining the "mind" of Christ as evidenced in an attitude of joy, gratitude, prayerfulness, sensitivity to the Holy Spirit, **discernment**, and **abstention** from every evil (1 Thessalonians 5:12-22); (6) protection for and careful **transmission** of the Word of God to those trained and able to teach others (2 Timothy 2:1,2); and (7) regular attendance at group worship (Hebrews 10:25).

The Church's Place in God's Prophetic Timeline

We have studied in past lessons God's 70 "sevens" or 490-year outline of Israel's final years before the fulfillment of all God's promises to her. We learned that there was a "gap" in that timeline, unknown to the Old Testament prophets, before the final seven years.

There are many views and opinions about how the church fits into the timeline of the final seven years. Some believe that the church will be "raptured" or caught up prior to this period. Others believe that the church will endure part of this time, usually defined as the first 3 1/2 years, and then be taken out. Still others believe that Christians will endure the entire tribulation period, meeting Christ as He returns with His heavenly host as the Mighty Conqueror. No one can know with certainty how and when these events will take place, and it is not the purpose of this study to draw rigid conclusions.

Regardless of how these events transpire, the number of years determined before the *"fullness of the Gentiles"* comes in, or the church age is over, is known only to God (Romans 11:25). Like the faithful Jewish bride, we are to wait—allowing no other to take His place in our affections—until He returns. Also, as the Body of Christ, we are to use our differing abilities to do the things that please Him while we wait, continually maintaining harmony within the "body" as we seek to reach the unsaved in all parts of the world. And, finally, as a building soundly constructed on the foundation of His perfect sacrifice, we can live at peace and without fear because the storms of this present ungodly world cannot destroy us as we work while we wait.

VOCABULARY

1. **abstention:** the act of holding off from using or doing something
2. **discernment:** the ability to perceive the distinctions, uniqueness, or clear value of or about something
3. **entity:** something that exists alone
4. **erring:** sinning or making a mistake
5. **evangelism:** the zealous preaching and spreading of the gospel
6. **nullify:** to counteract; to make void or useless
7. **submission:** the act of surrender to the authority of another; obedience to a superior
8. **transmission:** the act of sending or transferring something to another person or place

---

Notes

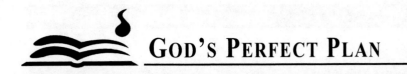
Daily Bible Study Questions

Study Procedure: Read the Scripture references before answering questions. Unless otherwise instructed, use the Bible only in answering questions. Some questions may be more difficult than others but try to answer as many as you can. Pray for God's wisdom and understanding as you study and don't be discouraged if some answers are not obvious at first.

FIRST DAY: Review of Lesson 13

1. On what foundation is the church built? (See 1 Corinthians 3:11.)

   Jesus Christ

2. List as many of the responsibilities of the church as you can from the previous lesson.

3. What mysteries were revealed in the last lesson?

4. Of these Scripture "pictures" of the church—Christ's body, Christ's bride, Christ's building—which is your favorite and why?

SECOND DAY:

5. In Bible studies, we often assume that every student is already a Christian, a member of the body of Christ. However, it is always important to review the basics—first to check ourselves and then to be be prepared to answer the questions of others. So, use this day's lesson as a potentially life-changing one as some basic salvation Scriptures are examined. Read and write out each verse and then answer the question asked about it.

   (a) (Romans 3:23)

(b) What has every single person done?

(c) (1 Peter 2:24)

(d) What is God's remedy for this?

(e) (Ephesians 2:8)

(f) How is this received? Is there any other way?

(g) (1 John 5:12)

(h) (Romans 8:16)

(i) How do you know if you have received it?

THIRD DAY:

6. Several events and judgments are associated with the return of Christ. One particular one called the *"judgment seat of Christ"* involves the church. Read these Scriptures that mention or allude to the *"judgment seat of Christ."* Then answer the questions that follow.

(Romans 14:10-12) *But why do you judge your brother? Or why do you show contempt for your brother? For we shall all stand before the judgment seat of Christ. For it is written: "As I live, says the LORD, every knee shall bow to Me, and every tongue shall confess to God." So then each of us shall give account of himself to God.*

(1 Corinthians 3:8-15) *"Now he who plants and he who waters are one, and each one will receive his own reward according to his own labor. For we are God's fellow workers; you are God's field, you are God's building. According to the grace of God which was given to me, as a wise master builder I have laid the foundation, and another builds on it. But let each one take heed how he builds on it. For no other foundation can anyone lay than that which is laid, which is Jesus Christ. Now if anyone builds on this foundation with gold, silver, precious stones, wood, hay, straw, each one's work will become clear; for*

the Day will declare it, because it will be revealed by fire; and the fire will test each one's work, of what sort it is. If anyone's work which he has built on it endures, he will receive a reward. If anyone's work is burned, he will suffer loss; but he himself will be saved, yet so as through fire."

(2 Corinthians 5:9,10) *"Therefore we make it our aim, whether present or absent, to be well pleasing to Him. For we must all appear before the judgment seat of Christ, that each one may receive the things done in the body, according to what he has done, whether good or bad."*

(1 Corinthians 4:5) *"Therefore judge nothing before the time, until the Lord comes, who will both bring to light the hidden things of darkness and reveal the counsels of the hearts. Then each one's praise will come from God."*

(Revelation 22:12) *"And behold, I am coming quickly, and My reward is with Me, to give to every one according to his work."*

(a) Who faces judgment in these passages?

(b) What is the purpose for the judgment?

(c) Who is the judge?

(d) God did not have to tell us ahead of time about this event, but He did. Comment on how this information might benefit a Christian in his present life?

FOURTH DAY:

7. Read the following passages and write down what you understand from each which assures the Christian that he will not be judged on the basis of his sins.
    (a) (Matthew 26:28) *"For this is My blood of the new covenant, which is shed for many for the remission of sins."*

    (b) (Acts 3:19) *"Repent therefore and be converted, that your sins may be blotted out, so that times of refreshing may come from the presence of the Lord...."*

(c) (Acts 10:43) *"To Him all the prophets witness that, through His name, whoever believes in Him will receive remission of sins."*

(d) (Acts 26:17,18) *"I will deliver you from the Jewish people, as well as from the Gentiles, to whom I now send you, to open their eyes, in order to turn them from darkness to light, and from the power of Satan to God, that they may receive forgiveness of sins and an inheritance among those who are sanctified by faith in Me."*

(e) (Ephesians 2:1-9) *"And you He made alive, who were dead in trespasses and sins, in which you once walked according to the course of this world, according to the prince of the power of the air, the spirit who now works in the sons of disobedience, among whom also we all once conducted ourselves in the lusts of our flesh, fulfilling the desires of the flesh and of the mind, and were by nature children of wrath, just as the others. But God, who is rich in mercy, because of His great love with which He loved us, even when we were dead in trespasses, made us alive together with Christ (by grace you have been saved), and raised us up together, and made us sit together in the heavenly places in Christ Jesus, that in the ages to come He might show the exceeding riches of His grace in His kindness toward us in Christ Jesus. For by grace you have been saved through faith, and that not of yourselves; it is the gift of God, not of works, lest anyone should boast."*

(f) (Hebrews 9:27,28) *"And as it is appointed for men to die once, but after this the judgment, so Christ was offered once to bear the sins of many. To those who eagerly wait for Him He will appear a second time, apart from sin, for salvation."*

(g) (1 John 1:9) *"If we confess our sins, He is faithful and just to forgive us our sins and to cleanse us from all unrighteousness."*

FIFTH DAY:

8. "Victor's" crowns are promised to believers as rewards for certain specific activities. Read the following Scriptures and then write what kind of "crown" is described and the action that merits it as explained in each passage.

(a) (1 Corinthians 9:25-27)

(b) (1 Thessalonians 2:17-20)

(c) (James 1:12)

(d) (2 Timothy 4:5-8)

(e) (1 Peter 5:2-4)

9. Are you a candidate for any of the above crowns? If you answered "yes," explain a current situation in which you have been used or tested in one or more of the above categories. If you answered "no," what do you intend to do about it?

MORE ABOUT THE CHURCH

Should We Still Go Out to All the World?

In a day when many main-line denominations are scaling down their missionary efforts abroad and questioning their "right to impose" Christianity on people of other belief systems, it is good for the Christian to ignore the pressure for political correctness and review some of the very basics of our faith. First of all, Jesus Himself issued the Great Commission of Matthew 28:16-20, and we must not ignore it. He said of Himself that He was the only way of salvation: *"I am the way, the truth, and the life. No one comes to the Father except through Me"* (John 14:6). Then Peter proclaimed the same truth leaving no room for any other way or plan: *"Nor is there salvation in any other, for there is no other name under heaven given among men by which we must be saved"* (Acts 4:12). When we fail to evangelize, we are leaving millions to face a final judgment without a Savior.

Examining Ourselves

Before going out to all the world, we must first make sure that we are truly members of the body of Christ ourselves. It is good to review the basic Scriptures about every person's need for a Savior and the provision made for that salvation through the death, resurrection, and ascension of Jesus Christ. It is quite sad that many who call themselves Christians are in reality not so at all. Some have mistakenly believed that if they have church membership that is enough. Others think that if their parents were Christians, they somehow inherited a saving faith. Still sadder are those who "act" Christian when in a Christian environment, but who quickly revert to an ungodly lifestyle when separated from more moral surroundings. The saddest of all, probably, are those who are working to earn salvation. They will be the most disappointed, as no person could ever do enough to earn what God only gives freely. In actuality, as seen from the Scriptures of the past lesson, there is no way to become a Christian except by accepting in faith that Christ did what the Bible said He did—took our place in judgment for our sins. In His name only is there salvation. He is the only way to get to God. That

truth is much too valuable to keep to ourselves. We must be about the business of telling others.

Coming Judgments

Several judgments are mentioned in the Bible, but only four really affect our coming study of the book of Revelation:

1. Judgment of believers at the *bema* or judgment seat of Christ (1 Corinthians 3:12-15).
2. Judgment of the nations at the beginning of Christ's reign at His return (Matthew 25:32).
3. Judgment of the earth during its whole course of history (2 Peter 3:5-7).
4. Judgment of the wicked dead at the end of Christ's reign on earth (Revelation 20:11,12).

Judgment Seat of Christ

As discovered in the questions section, a Christian does not have to answer for his sins at this judgment because they have been completely forgiven because of Christ's sacrifice. This *"judgment"* has to do with service or stewardship: what has been done with the opportunities or talents God has given. The original word for *"judgment seat"* used in Romans 14 and 2 Corinthians 5 was *bema*. This was the elevated platform or seat on which the judge of an athletic competition sat to observe or umpire a contest. To this platform the successful competitors came to receive their rewards. We see something quite similar in our modern-day Olympics. Often described as a race, the Christian life is an ongoing event in which each one must compete according to God's rules, persisting to the end, to receive the waiting rewards. So, the *bema* or judgment seat of Christ is a place of reward, not condemnation.

When will this *bema* judgment take place? Since it is not mentioned among the judgments in Revelation, many scholars believe it must take place while the "caught away" church is in heaven with Jesus before His return to the earth for the other final judgments. Just as a Jewish bride would be secluded with her groom for seven days so that he could get to know her intimately, sharing all her secrets, the church is likewise examined privately by Christ before she is revealed to the waiting public at the wedding feast. From the description in Revelation of the bride when she appears with Christ at His return, the *bema* seems to have already taken place.

> *And I heard, as it were, the voice of a great multitude, as the sound of many waters and as the sound of mighty thunderings, saying, "Alleluia! For the Lord God Omnipotent reigns! Let us be glad and rejoice and give Him glory, for the marriage of the Lamb has come, and His wife has made herself ready." And to her it was granted to be arrayed in fine linen, clean and bright, for the fine linen is the righteous acts of the saints* (Revelation 19:6-8).

The last judgment mentioned above, the judgment of the wicked dead at the end of Christ's reign on earth, will be discussed when we study Revelation 20.

Judgment of the Nations (Matthew 25:31-46)

In Matthew 24 and 25 Jesus answered His disciple's questions about the establishing of the kingdom prophesied for Israel. He explained to His disciples what would happen when He returned to them again in glory and power. Through clear statements (Matthew 24:36-44) and parables (Matthew 24:45-51 and Matthew 25:1-30) Jesus emphasized that only those prepared for His return could enter His kingdom. The indication is that Israel has had and will have had plenty of notice about what is required to enter the kingdom: faith in Him as Messiah and receiving of His Holy Spirit as a seal of that faith. When Jesus finally returns as prophesied, no excuses for failing to act on that truth will be accepted. A great separation will take place in which some of those alive at His return will be allowed to enter the kingdom because they have believed and obeyed what they had been told about Him, while others are sent away to everlasting punishment because they failed to do so.

In Matthew 25:31-46, Jesus changes His focus from the kingdom promised to Israel to the fate of the Gentiles (called here *"nations"*) who are alive at His return: *"When the Son of Man comes in His glory, and all the holy angels with Him, then He will sit on the throne of His glory. All the nations will be gathered before Him, and He will separate them one from another, as a shepherd divides his sheep from the goats..."* Although there is no place in Scripture that states that salvation is based on what a person does, in this descriptive parable, the actions of the *"sheep"* or *"goats"* seem to be evidence of their true spiritual condition. In the tribulation period, or last seven years of the present world, Israel will be under such terrible persecution that any Gentile feeding, clothing, or visiting *"the least of these My brethren"* will be risking his own life to do so. The parable seems to indicate that such actions are true indicators of a person's salvation, at least when Jesus—who can discern what is in a man—is doing the judging. Thus, the kind and unselfish *"sheep"* are welcomed into the Millennial kingdom while the selfish and unsaved *"goats"* are taken to *"everlasting punishment."* This judgment or separation is different from the Great White Throne of Judgment that will be discussed in Revelation 20. There the wicked dead of all the ages are resurrected and brought before Jesus for final judgment. In the Matthew 24 and 25 teachings, those wicked people alive at the return of Christ are separated and sent to their punishment so as to eliminate any unsaved persons from entering His Millennial kingdom.

Judgment of the Earth

In Revelation 21, right after Revelation 20's description of the Great White Throne Judgment, a *"new heaven and a new earth"* are shown to John. The first heaven and earth will have *"passed away."* The fact that the earth itself has "suffered" along with mankind ever since Adam and Eve first sinned and received the curse, has been made plain in Scripture. (See Romans 8:18-22.) When God judged mankind with the great Flood, the earth felt that judgment too: *"For this they willfully forget: that by the word of God the heavens were of old, and the earth standing out of water and in the water, by which the world that then existed perished, being flooded with water"* (2 Peter 3:5,6). Peter continued in this passage to describe a future judgment to be felt by the earth: *"But the heavens and the earth which now exist are kept in store by the same word, are reserved for fire until the day of judgment and perdition of ungodly men"* (2 Peter 3:7). Yes, Scripture teaches that while God remains forever, this present earth will come to an end and be changed: *"You, LORD, in the beginning laid the foundation of the earth, and the heavens are the work of Your hands. They will perish, but You remain; and they will all grow old like a garment; like a cloak You will fold them up, and they will be changed. But You are the same, and Your years will not fail"* (Hebrews 1:10-12). More discussion of this new heaven and earth for redeemed mankind will be discussed in Revelation 21.

Ready for Revelation

Starting with the very next lesson, we will spend the remainder of this course on a detailed study of the book of Revelation. All that has been studied thus far, the truths about God's plan for the nation of Israel, the place of the church in God's plans, and the part to be played by Gentile nations in the end-times, will prove valuable as we slowly examine the last days of our present world.

Notes

Notes

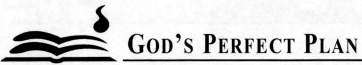

Daily Bible Study Questions

Study Procedure: Read the Scripture references before answering questions. Unless otherwise instructed, use the Bible only in answering questions. Some questions may be more difficult than others but try to answer as many as you can. Pray for God's wisdom and understanding as you study and don't be discouraged if some answers are not obvious at first.

FIRST DAY: Read Revelation 1:1-3

1. "Revelation" comes from a word meaning to pull back the curtain or to unveil something or someone. Who or what is being revealed in this book called "Revelation" ?

2. Outline the "process" God used to get this revelation to John.
   God > _____ > _____ > John

3. What other books of the Bible had John written and what were they about? (**Hint:** Look in the "Table of Contents" of your Bible or preface to each New Testament book.)

4. Which verse recorded a blessing on those who read and hear this prophecy and why do you think God promised such a blessing?

5. According to this passage, how soon could these things described in Revelation occur?

SECOND DAY: Read Revelation 1:4-8

6. Write the phrases that describe Jesus in verses 4-8 and give the number of the verse from which each phrase comes.

7. Choose at least two of the above phrases and explain what they mean in your own words.

8. What information is given in this chapter about the return of Christ to earth?

9. Read the following passages of Scripture. Underline any description of Christ's return that is similar to what you found above.
    (a) (Matthew 24:30) *"Then the sign of the Son of Man will appear in heaven, and then all the tribes of the earth will mourn, and they will see the Son of Man coming on the clouds of heaven with power and great glory."*

    (b) (Matthew 26:64) *Jesus said to him, "It is as you said. Nevertheless, I say to you, hereafter you will see the Son of Man sitting at the right hand of the Power, and coming on the clouds of heaven."*

    (c) (Mark 13:26) *"Then they will see the Son of Man coming in the clouds with great power and glory."*

    (d) (Zechariah 12:10) *"And I will pour on the house of David and on the inhabitants of Jerusalem the Spirit of grace and supplication; then they will look on Me whom they pierced. Yes, they will mourn for Him as one mourns for his only son, and grieve for Him as one grieves for a firstborn."*

THIRD DAY: Read Revelation 1:9-20

10. (a) Where was John at this time?

    (b) Why was he there?

    (c) What was he instructed to do?

11. Read John's description of the vision of Jesus (Revelation 1:12-20). Describe the following and explain the significance of each, if you can.
    (a) His clothing

(b) hair

(c) eyes

(d) feet

(e) voice

(f) mouth

(g) countenance

(h) what He was holding

12. What was John's reaction to seeing Jesus?

13. Read the following passages and summarize the reactions of these persons when they saw the Lord.
(a) Isaiah (Isaiah 6:1-8)

(b) Ezekiel (Ezekiel 1:28)

(c) Paul (Acts 9:1-9)

FOURTH DAY:

14. Many students of Revelation believe that Revelation 1:19 is the outline for the entire book. What would be its three main divisions?

   I.

   II.

   III.

15. How was the symbolism of the stars and lampstands explained?

16. Why do you think symbols were used rather than a literal description or explanation? (See Matthew 13:10-17.)

FIFTH DAY:

17. See if you can match each number with its symbolic meaning.

   one   two   three   four   five   six   seven   eight   ten   twelve   forty

   _____ (a) the earth or world (Isaiah 11:12)
   _____ (b) perfection (Psalm 12:6; Revelation 3:1)
   _____ (c) God (Deuteronomy 6:4)
   _____ (d) This and double this stand for human completion. (**Hint:** senses, fingers, moral law)
   _____ (e) the minimum number of witnesses needed to establish the truth (Deuteronomy 19:15)
   _____ (f) the number representing Father, Son, and Holy Spirit
   _____ (g) man (Revelation 13:18)
   _____ (h) number of testing, waiting, or preparation (Exodus 16:35; 24:18)
   _____ (i) new beginning (Genesis 17:12; 1 Peter 3:20)
   _____ (j) God's governmental number (Numbers 1:44; Mark 3:14)

THE REVELATION OF JESUS CHRIST

Pulling Back the Curtain

A preacher once said that whenever he became a bit nervous or discouraged about the state of the world around him, he took comfort in skipping to the end of "God's Book"—the Bible—to see how it ends: Revelation tells us that God wins! The final book of the Bible (from the Greek word *apokalypsis*, meaning "to unveil or pull back the curtain") repeats the earlier promises and prophecies about Jesus' dramatic return to earth. At that time, the whole world will see Him, and every person, alive or dead, who has accepted His gift of salvation by faith, will be absolutely secure in their eternal place with Him in the world to come. This final outcome is important for every student of Revelation to keep in mind in order to avoid becoming fearful at some of the specific and often terrifying details given about the last years on earth before Jesus' return.

Four Views

As you have probably already discovered, not every Christian agrees on how to study or understand Revelation. Four common views are explained briefly below:

1. Preterist View: This comes from a word (preterite) which is used to describe a tense of a verb which signifies completed past. This view holds that everything in Revelation was fulfilled around the time that John recorded the visions he was given. This is not a very popular view, since historical events at that time do not seem to fulfill in any clear way the prophecies given.

2. Historical View: This view holds that the events of Revelation occurred during the last many centuries of the existence of the church. Again, this does not follow the clear meaning of Scripture and is not backed up by chronological or historical facts.

3. Spiritual View: This was a popular view before the 1900's when the world was optimistic about man's improvement and had hope for making the world a much better place. It holds that everything in Revelation should be taken figuratively or metaphorically as if the events recorded or prophesied were meant to give the overall truth of the conflict of good and evil. Those holding this view felt that there would not be a real time of tribulation or judgment and no necessity for Christ to actually come and rule the world for a thousand years because man's goodness would usher in peace for the world. However, after two world wars and numerous other setbacks to the hopes for the goodness of man, people have left this view.

4. Futurist View: The view held by this author is this one. It is made of the belief that the activities described in Revelation are primarily for future fulfillment, especially after chapter four. The words of these prophecies in this view are taken literally except where the context and facts of the passage or subject matter suggest the contrary.

Aids to Understanding Revelation

Keep these things in mind when studying Revelation:

1. A helpful rule suggested by Dr. David L. Cooper and quoted on page 3 of Dr. Tim LaHaye's *Revelation* was this: "When the plain sense of Scripture makes common sense, seek no other sense; therefore, take every word at its primary, ordinary, usual, literal, meaning unless the facts of the immediate text, studied in the light of related passages and…fundamental truths, clearly indicate otherwise."

2. Identify where the scene takes place. In Revelation, the scene switches back and forth between heaven and earth and to different locations on the earth. The setting of a passage is important in determining the meaning.

3. Not everything in Revelation is recorded chronologically. Basic "signposts" to identify where in the seven-year period a scene is, will be offered along with the study of later chapters.

John the Apostle

John, one of the original twelve disciples, wrote Revelation in his final years. Many Bible researchers place his age at about ninety when he was exiled by Rome's emperor to the island of **Patmos** for preaching the gospel message. While his enemies hoped to keep him quiet and ineffective, God had other plans. John had already written one of the four Gospel accounts and three of the epistles, but God allowed him to receive this last dramatic vision of the future of the world and trusted him to record what he was shown. John's final work was really the record of a series of visions given to him while he was *"in the Spirit on the Lord's day."* The *"Lord's day"* is commonly thought to refer to the first day of the week, our Sunday, on which the church—over time—became accustomed to using for a day of worship. However, other Bible scholars believe it refers to the *"day of the Lord"* and indicates that John received a vision of God's plans for a future time period. The important thing to see, however, is not what day of the week it was, but that the Holy Spirit was pulling back the curtain of the future for John and showing him the events leading up to and including the end of the world.

Centuries before, God had revealed some of these same things to another of his servants named Daniel. So, the plans God had for the last days were not new ideas but carefully planned and ordered events. The whole "revelation" exposes the depths of evil to which man will finally sink in his determination to live apart from God. However, it also reveals the wonderful provision God has made for those who love Him. John was faithful to record what he was shown, and we are promised a blessing for our efforts in reading and understanding what he recorded.

The Uniqueness of Revelation

Revelation is the only New Testament book completely dedicated to prophecy. As John stretched our imaginations by going all the way back to Creation in his gospel [*"In the beginning was the Word...."* (John 1:1)], he pushed our thoughts ahead—deep into the future—in Revelation. Nothing new is introduced in Revelation; every "big idea" had its beginning somewhere else in Scripture. More than half of the verses of Revelation (274 out of 404) refer or **allude** to the Old Testament. The Holy Spirit brought the many different strands of prophetic information from the Old and New Testaments together here, weaving them into a pattern that can be recognized and understood by the careful Bible student.

The Purpose of the Book (Revelation 1:1-3)

From God's mind to Jesus' through angels to John, the future was unveiled—*"things which must shortly take place."* The word *"must"* emphasizes that God has decided and everything will certainly occur as He has explained. *"Shortly"* has the meaning of "suddenly or quickly," meaning that once these things begin to happen, they will continue without interruption or delay. A blessing is promised to those who read, hear, and keep the words of Revelation. Part of the blessing is peace of mind. God wants His children to know where the world is headed so that they will not be afraid of the future but, instead, continue to trust and obey Him as the Lord of all. He wants them to be able to recognize the work of Satan and the worldwide trouble he will cause in his final assault against the kingdom of God.

The Address of the Revelation (Revelation 1:4-8)

John was told to record this series of visions for seven specific **Asian** churches. According to archeological information, the order in which these city-churches were listed was exactly that of a Roman postal route in John's day. (Note: Refer to Lesson 16 page 56 for a map of these churches.) John was probably personally familiar with the members of each church in that area, having lived and preached longer than any other of the original disciples of Jesus before his exile on Patmos. Although they were actual churches, they were used to represent all churches in all ages, and the messages given to them still apply to our own congregations.

The Announcement (Revelation 1:7,8)

Jesus will return to earth! This announcement or prophecy had been given hundreds of times in the Old and New Testaments, and here the event is once more described:

1. It is actual. This is not a parable or symbol. Jesus will actually return to earth.

2. It is personal. Every single person living on the earth at that time will see Him—even those who pierced Him. This is a reference to Israel. (See Zechariah 12:10.) No one will miss this event. How people respond to what they see will depend on whether or not they accepted the opportunity to know Him at His first coming. Many will not rejoice but, instead, will mourn because of their earlier rejection of Him.

3. It is visible. He will be clearly seen, coming in the clouds from heaven. He will be recognized as Jesus Christ who *"loved us and washed us from our sins in His own blood"* (verse 5) and yet one who now has *"glory and dominion forever and ever"* (verse 6).

In the Spirit

While John was *"in the Spirit on the Lord's Day"* he heard a loud trumpet-like voice announcing the identity of a spectacular Person. The Person was Jesus Himself, not the crucified Savior but the Omnipotent Sovereign! *"In the Spirit"* meant that John had made himself available to hear from God that particular day. He might have been praying or just waiting on God to speak to him. To be *"in the Spirit,"* one must quiet the "flesh"—all the wandering thoughts, nervous movements, or unnecessary activities that drown out the voice of God. Do you allow regular *"in the Spirit"* time-outs to study, pray, or listen to God?

The Vision of Jesus (Revelation 1:9-18)

It is important to consider the first vision John was given in this book. It was a vision of *"One like the Son of Man."* Jesus applied that term to Himself many times, as recorded in all four gospels, and Stephen identified Him with that term when he saw Him shortly before he was martyred in Acts 7. God, first and foremost, wanted us to see Jesus in this revelation of the last days, for truly *"the testimony of Jesus is the spirit of prophecy"* (Revelation 19:10). Not the crucified Jesus here, however, but the Jesus risen and ruling Lord of heaven. This should encourage us because it shows, from first to last, Jesus is in control. John even described this inclusive role when he called Jesus the *"Alpha and the Omega, the First and the Last"* (verse 11). Alpha and omega are the first and last letters of the Greek alphabet and depict Jesus' power from beginning to end.

How He Looked

Using symbolic description, John explained what he was seeing. In the middle of seven lampstands stood Jesus dressed in a long garment and golden chest band like a priest or king. Appropriate to His great wisdom and maturity, His head and hair were *"white like wool"* (verse 14). The powerful all-seeing eyes were described as being *"like a flame of fire."* No power could stop or turn this Son of Man with feet like fine brass. Brass was the metal used for the altar in the Old Testament and is a metal that can endure great heat. It is associated with judgment, and so Jesus is seen as the one with the power and authority to judge the world. His voice was as powerful as rushing waters, while out of His mouth came a sharp two-edged sword. There is no need to guess as to that meaning. In Hebrews 4:12, that is the description given to the word of God. The two edges indicate effectiveness at all times as well as a dual purpose: to heal or to punish. John ended the description with the comment that the face of the Son of Man shined like the sun.

Appropriate Awe

John *"fell at His feet as dead"* when he was given this vision of his all-powerful Lord (verse 17). Similarly, so had Isaiah, Ezekiel, and even Paul when confronted with a similar vision. We often fail to realize the greatness of our Lord and are guilty of becoming overly familiar when thinking of, speaking to, or approaching Him. We would do well to ponder John's image and take pains to approach Him with a reverence due His high position.

Helpful Outline (Revelation 1:19)

Many have seen in Revelation 1:19 an outline for the book of Revelation:

1. Things which you have seen: the vision of the omnipotent Son of Man, Chapter 1.

2. Things which are: the message to the seven churches, Chapters 2 and 3.

3. Things which will take place after this: the last seven years, after the church age, Chapters 4-22.

Stars and Lampstands: Why Use Symbols? (Revelation 1:20)

The symbolism used throughout Revelation makes it a challenging book for any Bible student. Why did God choose to use so much symbolic description? The disciples asked Jesus the same thing about His frequent use of symbolism and parable instead of straightforward plain language: *"And the disciples came and said to Him, 'Why do You speak to them in parables?' He answered and said to them, 'Because it has been given to you to know the mysteries of the kingdom of heaven, but to them it has not been given'"* (Matthew 13:10,11). As encoded messages are still used by our military forces in order to keep vital information from our enemies while informing our own troops, God protected the message of Revelation from people outside the covenant, while informing His own "troops" so that they could be prepared. The meanings of symbols can best be learned from Scripture itself. Just as Hebrews 4:12 explained the *"two-edged sword,"* so right in this chapter John explained the lampstands and stars: The lampstands are the churches and the stars represent the angels or ministers of those churches. Jesus is closely involved with both, as will be seen in the next lesson.

Use Numbers to Teach

Not just in Revelation, but throughout the Bible, numbers are often used to add another layer of meaning to the passages in which they occur. Below is a short summary of the meanings of numbers when used in the Bible in symbolic ways.

One: From earliest days, the verse in Deuteronomy 6:4 called the *Shema*, associated this number with God alone: *"Hear, O Israel: The LORD our God, the LORD is one!"*

Two: According to Deuteronomy 19:15, this was the minimum number needed to establish the truth:

"One witness shall not rise against a man concerning any iniquity or any sin that he commits; by the mouth of two or three witnesses the matter shall be established." Two, then, is the number of witness.

Three: This number represents the Holy Trinity for Christians.

Four: This number is associated with the earth: *"He will set up a banner for the nations, and will assemble the outcasts of Israel, and gather together the dispersed of Judah from the four corners of the earth"* (Isaiah 11:12). There are four seasons and four points to the compass.

Five and Ten: These are often used to emphasize something that is complete, according to the human idea, such as ten fingers or toes or the five senses. In Revelation, there will be ten-member confederation of nations that gives power to the Beast. When God gave the laws whereby man would be governed, He gave them in the form of ten commandments. When God freed Israel from Egypt, He used ten plagues to break Pharaoh's human strength and will.

Six: Six is one less than seven and is given in Revelation as the number of man—lower than God. Man was created on the sixth day. When repeated three times, it also becomes the representation of the unholy trinity of Satan, the Antichrist, and the false prophet: *"Here is wisdom. Let him who has understanding calculate the number of the beast, for it is the number of a man: His number is 666"* (Revelation 13:18).

Seven: This number is symbolic of perfection or completion. These references help in understanding it: *"The words of the LORD are pure words, like silver tried in a furnace of earth, purified seven times"* (Psalm 12:6). *"And from the throne proceeded lightnings, thunderings, and voices. Seven lamps of fire were burning before the throne, which are the seven Spirits of God"* (Revelation 4:5).

Eight: Eight is the number of the new beginning. This was the number of persons God used to "start over" after the flood: *"...who formerly were disobedient, when once the Divine longsuffering* *waited in the days of Noah, while the ark was being prepared, in which a few, that is, eight souls, were saved through water"* (1 Peter 3:20). It was also the day of circumcision, when a Jewish baby boy would receive the sign of the covenant: *"He who is eight days old among you shall be circumcised, every male child in your generations, he who is born in your house or bought with money from any foreigner who is not your descendant"* (Genesis 17:12). And the eighth day on a calendar is the start of a new week as the eighth note in a musical scale is the start of a new octave.

Twelve: This number represents the government or system of organization that God has chosen—like the twelve tribes of Israel or the twelve disciples (Numbers 1:44; Mark 3:14).

Forty: This number is associated with waiting or testing. *"And the children of Israel ate manna forty years, until they came to an inhabited land; they ate manna until they came to the border of the land of Canaan"* (Exodus 16:35). *"So Moses went into the midst of the cloud and went up into the mountain. And Moses was on the mountain forty days and forty nights"* (Exodus 24:18).

Most of these numbers will appear in Revelation and this brief explanation should help in understanding their significance.

VOCABULARY

1. **allude:** to make indirect reference to
2. **Asian:** this area would now be in what we know as Turkey, north of the Mediterranean Sea
3. **Patmos:** an island situated off the southwest coast of Turkey in the Aegean Sea; It is a rocky treeless island, about ten miles long and six miles wide.

Notes

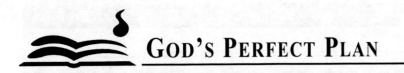

Daily Bible Study Questions

Study Procedure: Read the Scripture references before answering questions. Unless otherwise instructed, use the Bible only in answering questions. Some questions may be more difficult than others but try to answer as many as you can. Pray for God's wisdom and understanding as you study and don't be discouraged if some answers are not obvious at first.

FIRST DAY: Review of Lesson 15

1. What does "revelation" mean?

2. Why do we as Christians need to know about God's future plans for the world?

3. About what in Revelation are you looking forward to studying?

4. Give the outline of Revelation from Revelation 1:19.

5. **Map Review:** Place a number by each city-church on the map on the next page to indicate how it is listed in Revelation 1:11 and discussed in Chapters 2 and 3. This order is believed to be the same as the postal route of that time.

6. Find Patmos on the map and circle it.

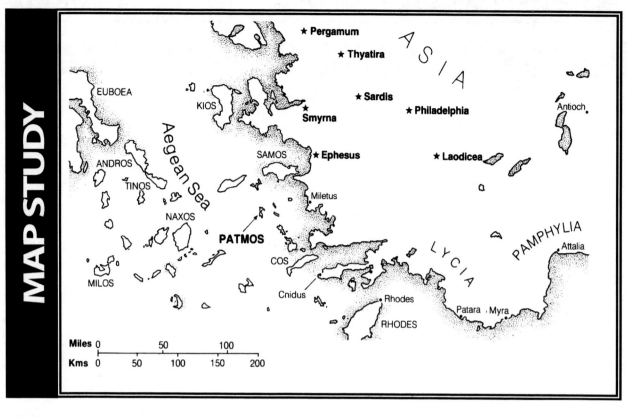

SECOND DAY: Read Revelation 1:20 and 2:1-7

7. Why would a lampstand (literally, oil lamp) be an appropriate symbol for a church? (See Matthew 5:14.)

8. The seven stars which Jesus held in His right hand (Revelation 1:20) were explained as being angels. The word for angels is literally "messengers." What are some possibilities for who these "messengers" were?

9. Read Revelation 2:1-7 and fill in this chart with the appropriate information about the church at Ephesus.

Compliment	Criticism	Advice	Promise

10. What was this church told specifically to do if it were to return to its *"first love"* for Christ?

11. What sort of things could cause a Christian or even an entire church to leave their *"first love"* for Christ?

THIRD DAY: Read Revelation 2:8-17

12. Fill in this chart with the appropriate information about Smyrna from Revelation 2:8-11.

Compliment	Criticism	Advice	Promise

13. Smyrna's name was related in meaning to the burial spice called myrrh, one of the prophetically appropriate gifts given to Jesus by the wise men at His birth. Smyrna is a church that had to undergo much suffering for her faith in Jesus. With this information, what was meaningful about the way Christ identified Himself to them in verse 8?

14. Was her suffering going to stop right away? Support your answer with Scripture.

15. Fill in the chart below about Pergamos from Revelation 2:12-17.

Compliment	Criticism	Advice	Promise

16. Choose the best description from the following list for the church at Pergamos and then give your reasons for doing so.

cowardly   compromising   caring   cold

FOURTH DAY: Read Revelation 2:18-3:13

17. Complete the chart for Thyatira from Revelation 2:18-29.

Compliment	Criticism	Advice	Promise

18. Christ is identified in verse 18 as coming with *"eyes like a flame of fire, and...feet like fine brass."* That speaks of His role as righteous Judge. What or who is judged in this letter and what is the verdict and sentence?

19. From Revelation 3:1-6, fill out the chart for Sardis.

Compliment	Criticism	Advice	Promise

20. Jesus, who has complete or perfect spiritual knowledge (*"seven Spirits of God"*), saw through the outward appearance of the church at Sardis. If a church today had a name for being *"alive"* but was really spiritually *"dead,"* what might it look like to us or to the world?

21. Complete the chart for Philadelphia from Revelation 3:7-13.

Compliment	Criticism	Advice	Promise

FIFTH DAY: Continue in Revelation 3:7-13; Read Revelation 3:14-22

22. The description of Jesus in verse 7 is as One *"who has the key of David, He who opens and no one shuts, and shuts and no one opens."* This was followed by Jesus describing an opportunity to the church at Philadelphia. What was it and why were they given it?

23. What else is promised them because of their perseverance?

24. Read Revelation 3:14-22 and fill in the form below about the church at Laodicea.

Compliment	Criticism	Advice	Promise

25. This church thought they had it all, but they didn't! In fact, according to verse 20, what was the real cause of their lukewarmness and spiritual blindness?

26. Now imagine Jesus was speaking to your church. As you did above, write down what you think He would say.

Compliment	Criticism	Advice	Promise

27. Review the charts of the seven churches.
    (a) Which church did not receive a compliment?

    (b) Which church(es) did not receive a criticism?

THE SEVEN CHURCHES

The Things That Are

John had been preaching the gospel for many years before his exile on Patmos and had probably visited the seven churches listed in these chapters many times. All seven were actual cities with actual churches at the time John recorded the visions of Revelation. Some Bible students see in the messages given and the characteristics described an outline of each major era of church history. For example, since the testing of apostles is mentioned in the letter to Ephesus in Revelation 2:2, some see her as the first century church, which had begun enthusiastically at Pentecost but had become weary of spiritual struggles and religious **confrontation,** eventually leaving her *"first love."* Smyrna represents a period of terrible persecution of the church by Rome and others, from AD 100 to AD 312. Next, Pergamos represents for some the era when Christianity had been made acceptable through Emperor Constantine's **edicts** and as such was soon dulled by worldliness and allowed to mix its truths with the deceptions of Satan. Beginning at about AD 600 and running through at least 1500, Thyatira is seen to represent the church in the Dark Ages. Instead of leaving her *"first love,"* this era saw the church more active at the end than the beginning, but she was still **riddled** with false teaching which led multitudes to spiritual death. Continuing this pattern, Sardis represents the churches of the Reformation era, beginning about 1520. They did much good at first, but later evolved into state-run churches which were spiritually more dead than alive. Philadelphia, the church praised by Christ, represents for some the era beginning about 1750, when out of the dead state-churches, reformers prayed and worked for revival, which did begin in Europe and swept even to America. Laodicea is the *"lukewarm"* church, representing a period which began about the 1900's, when the teaching of evolution began taking root to undermine the truth of the Genesis account of Creation and subsequently all Scripture. Philadelphia and Laodicea are seen by some as continuing their existence now and on through to the Rapture.

While some Bible authorities enjoy explaining some form of the above pattern of church history, this interpretation cannot be defended too fiercely. After all, each of the characteristics of these seven churches could be identified today in churches all over the world, and, sadly, probably in every town in our nation as well.

Many scholars dismiss the view of church eras being represented by the Asian churches. They see that in the selection of just seven, out of all the many existing churches at that time, God was seeking to give His children a representation of what was right or wrong in any church in any age. The number seven can mean "complete," as well as "perfect," and so to those holding this second view, the Asian churches represent the complete range of the conditions existing in churches the world over. We should learn from their successes and failures, and repent accordingly.

Remembering the Seven

You will probably find it helpful to invent a code or memory-aid for listing the seven churches. Try this one: Every Smile Proves That Saints Promote Love.

Every: Ephesus
Smile: Smyrna
Proves: Pergamos
That: Thyatira
Saints: Sardis
Promote: Philadelphia
Love: Laodicea

Ephesus (Revelation 2:1-7)

For two years the apostle Paul had taught those at Ephesus and established that place as a strong center for Christian work and teaching (Acts 19:1-10). After Paul's death, John became a leader there. Ephesus was located on the western coast of what was then called Asia. It had been an important center for commerce and culture since the time of Alexander the Great, being benefited by the Roman road system which terminated there. It was known as the home for one of the wonders of the ancient world, the temple of the heathen goddess Artemis.

In this letter to Ephesus, Jesus told them that He was aware of their works, patience, and intolerance of evil men or false leaders (Revelation 2:2). However, they had *"left"* their *"first love."* Note that He did not say they had "lost" their first love. Love is not a feeling, though it certainly can be accompanied by feelings, but a decision. Feelings fluctuate while decisions should stand. As they had at some point "decided" not to be as enthusiastic in their discipleship, so they could repent—change their minds—and decide again to go back to the things they had done when their faith was fresh. Without sincere godly service, a church does not "light" the way for others. Jesus said firmly that without a change, their *"lampstand"* would be removed *"from its place."* This is a strong warning for any church that has relaxed its earlier obedient efforts in evangelism and disciple-making.

The Nicolaitans are mentioned in this letter (Revelation 2:6) as well as in the letter to Pergamos (Revelation 2:15). The identity of the Nicolaitans, their leader, or their beliefs are not exactly known now. They could have been followers of a leader by that name or a group that "conquered the laity" (the literal meaning of that word) by allowing idolatry, sexual immorality, or other *"deeds"* that Jesus hated to be allowed in the church (Revelation 2:6). At least the Ephesian church had not relaxed their love for Christ enough to allow that.

With a final reminder to hear *"what the Spirit says to the churches,"* Jesus promised the overcomers —John's synonym for real Christians (see 1 John 5:4,5)—that they will eat of the tree of life. The reverse of the curse on Eden is promised and a residence for Christians in the Paradise of God has been prepared.

Smyrna (Revelation 2:8-11)

Smyrna is often called the suffering church. They were poor because of persecution by people who claimed to be righteous Jews. Jesus said that in His eyes they were rich, and that those persecuting them were not righteous at all, but of the *"synagogue of Satan."* Smyrna was north of Ephesus and competed with that city for commerce and cultural contributions. One famous Christian to come out of that church was Polycarp, Smyrna's

bishop, who was burned at the stake in AD 156. Foxe's *Book of the Martyrs* records the following information about his martyrdom, which exemplifies the spirit of the persecuted church so praised by Jesus in this letter:

Hearing his captors had arrived one evening, Polycarp left his bed to welcome them, ordered a meal prepared for them and then asked for an hour alone to pray. The soldiers were so impressed by Polycarp's advanced age and composure that they began to wonder why they had been sent to take him, but as soon as he had finished his prayers, they put him on an ass and brought him to the city.

As he entered the stadium with his guards, a voice from heaven was heard to say, "Be strong, Polycarp, and play the man." No one nearby saw anyone speaking, but many people heard the voice. Brought before the tribunal and the crowd, Polycarp refused to deny Christ, although the proconsul begged him to "consider yourself and have pity on your great age. Reproach Christ and I will release you." Polycarp replied, "Eighty-six years I have served Him, and He never once wronged me. How can I blaspheme my King who saved me?" Threatened with wild beasts and fire, Polycarp stood his ground. "What are you waiting for? Do whatever you please." The crowd demanded Polycarp's death, gathering wood for the fire and preparing to tie him to the stake. "Leave me," he said. "He who will give me strength to sustain the fire will help me not to flinch from the pile." So they bound him but didn't nail him to the stake. As soon as Polycarp finished his prayer, the fire was lit, but it leaped up around him, leaving him unburned, until the people convinced a soldier to plunge a sword into him (to kill him). When he did, so much blood gushed out that the fire was immediately extinguished. The soldiers then placed his body into a fire and burned it to ashes, which some Christians later gathered up and buried properly.

The believers at Smyrna were told not to fear what they were about to suffer because God had limited the suffering to *"ten days."* This could mean just what it says—a coming persecution faced by this church at the time of the letter would only last ten days. However, if ten is the number of human completion, it could symbolize a limited period of persecution, mercifully halted by God.

The promise of this letter to the saved or *"he who overcomes"* was that they would not be hurt by the *"second death."* What is the *"second death"*? The first death is the natural death of the body that faces everyone: *"And as it is appointed for men to die once, but after this the judgment..."* (Hebrews 9:27). The second death will be spiritual separation from God because the person refused to accept salvation through Jesus. There is a saying, "Born twice, die once, but born once, die twice." Being born again in Christ stops the *"second death."*

Pergamos (Revelation 2:12-17)

Pergamos (Pergamum) was north of Smyrna and about 15 miles inland from the Aegean Sea. It was not as important a commercial center as Ephesus and Smyrna, but had great fame as a religious center. There, worship of the Roman emperor was highly promoted as well as participation in temple worship for Zeus, Athena, Dionysius, and Asklepios. Zeus' temple was set on a hill about 800 feet above the city, making it a dramatic **spectacle**. Probably because of all this idolatry, sexual immorality associated with it, and the pressure to publicly worship the emperor and deny Christ, Jesus called this place *"Satan's throne."* He commended Pergamos Christians for holding strong to their confession of faith in Him even when threatened with death, as in the case of a martyr named Antipas. The introduction of Jesus in this letter as *"He who has the sharp two-edged sword"* puts Him in contrast to the power of Rome, which also ruled with a sword. Jesus' sword, of course, was in all ways superior and effective even to the separation of what was true and false (Hebrews 4:12). Jesus' correction of them had to do with their failure to oppose the sins of the Nicolaitans as Ephesus had. Pergamos had allowed false teaching to go on without stopping it. Reread Numbers 22-25 to understand the comparison to Israel's most famous false teacher Balaam and the

problems he caused for Israel. Jesus urged them to repent, reminding them of His sword which would fight on their behalf. The promise to the "overcomers" or the saved this time was for *"hidden manna."* This was representative of the *"bread of life"* Jesus gives to those who love Him. The *"white stone"* engraved with *"a new name"* has been thought to refer to the Roman practice of using white stones to vote "innocent" in a trial or to the use of them as tickets to enter a feast or other event. In any case, faith in Christ brings new identity and special privileges.

Thyatira (Revelation 2:18-29)

Thyatira was about forty miles southeast of Pergamos, on the border of the region then called Mysia. While it was not famous for heathen temples, it was a place where trade **guilds** were powerful influences on society. To work effectively and profitably, it was necessary to belong to one of these guilds. Pressure to belong, then as now, caused some to "go along" with practices that were not godly. Thyatira was known for its production of an expensive purple dye. Lydia of Acts 16:14 was a seller of purple from Thyatira. Jesus with *"eyes like a flame of fire"* and *"feet like fine brass"* exhibited His clear vision of what was good and bad about this church. On the positive side, He recognized their *"love, service, faith,...patience"* and that these works had even increased: *"the last are more than the first."* However, their failure to put an end to the **seductive** teachings of a woman, who was probably sarcastically called Jezebel (see 1 Kings 16-21), made Jesus confront them about the spiritual damage which resulted. He would judge both her and all those who followed her (called here *"her children"*) with death, unless they repented. Those not guilty of following her doctrine, were urged to *"hold fast what you have till I come."* The blessing for the saved here was the right to rule with Jesus over the nations and receive the *"morning star."*

Sardis (Revelation 3:1-6)

Sardis was a busy commercial and industrial city located about thirty miles southeast of Thyatira. Wool was an important industry for Sardis and it was served by five Roman roads as sort of a hub of the region. It had an almost **impregnable** fortress on a high hill which gave it perhaps a false sense of security. While mention is made of a *"few names"* who had remained faithful to God, overall Sardis is condemned for having a reputation for being alive, while they were actually spiritually dead as a church. Jesus, described as having the *"seven Spirits of God,"* most likely a reference to the perfection of the Holy Spirit, was able to "see through" the false image of the Sardis church. His advice was to repent and then strengthen what was left that was good. The promise to the Christians here, was to be clothed in *"white garments,"* symbolic of right standing with God and the righteous deeds of the saints (Revelation 19:8). They were also guaranteed that their names would not be blotted out of the *"Book of Life"* but instead confessed before God and the angels.

Philadelphia (Revelation 3:7-13)

Philadelphia was in the province of Lydia and about thirty miles southeast of Sardis. The city was on a plateau made rich by volcanic soil. The grape industry was the most profitable, and so the worship of Dionysius was promoted. Jesus, identified as the one with the *"key of David"* who can open and shut without being challenged, offers an open door to Philadelphia. In spite of their *"little strength,"* they had kept His word and not denied His name. Their main struggle was with supposedly religious Jews. However, Jesus said they were not good Jews but members of the *"synagogue of Satan."* He promised the church at Philadelphia that He would humble their enemies, allowing them to recognize His love for His church. The reward for their perseverance was to escape from the *"hour of trial which shall come upon the whole world, to test those who dwell on the earth."* This is often quoted to support the belief that the church will not go through the seven-year tribulation period that is described in the remaining chapters of Revelation. In a city often plagued by earthquakes, Jesus promised to make them like secure pillars in His temple, giving them His own new name. Philadelphia, like Smyrna, received no criticism from Jesus.

Laodicea (Revelation 3:14-22)

Laodicea was the final church on the route of the seven. It was in a valley of the Lycus River and was reached by three different Roman roads. That helped its commercial importance. Sheep-growing—specializing in black wool—helped promote clothing and carpet industries as well. Laodicea was a wealthy city, independent of welfare from Rome, and was famous for an effective eye medicine. Jesus, introduced in this letter as the *"Amen"* or finisher of God's plans, as well as the Creator of all, condemned this self-sufficient church for being lukewarm and nauseating to Him. They were blind to their real condition. They didn't think they needed anything from God because they were wealthy, strong, well-clothed, medically secure, and happy. He said that they needed to come to Him for the things that were eternal: spiritual *"gold refined in the fire,"* white garments of righteousness instead of the black wool of which they were so proud, and spiritual eye salve so that they could really see the truth about themselves and God. He reminded them that He only rebuked and chastened those He loved, and then urged them to *"be zealous and repent."* The most famous verse in this passage is verse 20, where Jesus says that He is outside their door, knocking, and waiting to be invited in. What a tragic picture of the church even in our day! We have left Jesus outside, thinking we could do everything very well ourselves. How foolish! To the ones able to overcome such false beliefs, Jesus promised a place with Him and His Father on their thrones.

Final Warning

One more time, Jesus warned the churches to listen to what He had told them: *"He who has an ear, let him hear what the Spirit says to the churches."* Have you been listening? Of what do you and your church need to repent? Pray about it and act on what you know you need to do while these letters are fresh on your mind and heart. He will help His own to "overcome" this world, the flesh, and the devil.

VOCABULARY

1. **confrontation:** face to face meeting, usually over differences
2. **edicts:** proclamations; orders; commands
3. **guilds:** organizations joining together people with the same trade or occupation
4. **impregnable:** impossible to enter or conquer
5. **riddled:** perforated with numerous holes
6. **seductive:** attempting to draw away from proper conduct
7. **spectacle:** a public display of something unusual

Notes

Daily Bible Study Questions

Study Procedure: Read the Scripture references before answering questions. Unless otherwise instructed, use the Bible only in answering questions. Some questions may be more difficult than others but try to answer as many as you can. Pray for God's wisdom and understanding as you study and don't be discouraged if some answers are not obvious at first.

FIRST DAY: Review of Lesson 16

1. Identify the church from the description and give a reference with your answer.
   (a) This is the persecuted church.

   (b) This church had given an open-door to service and was faithful.

   (c) This lukewarm church thought they were rich, healthy, and stylish, but they were really poor, blind and naked.

   (d) This church was dead.

   (e) The last works are better than the first in this church, but Jezebel should have been stopped.

   (f) This compromising church allowed false teaching to continue although they had been faithful to stand against some of Satan's attacks.

   (g) This church needed to go back to their first works; they had left their first love.

2. What was most meaningful to you from either the notes or lecture last week.

SECOND DAY: Read Revelation 4

3. Revelation 4:1 begins, *"After these things."* To what do you think that refers—in other words, after what things?

4. What was the timeframe in which he was to understand this vision of Chapter 4 ?

5. From the opening verses of Chapter 4, what was John shown at this time?

6. Instead of details of God's physical form, John gives a description full of color, sound, and glory. Match the following things to what they referred or described:

   _____ (a) a rainbow
   _____ (b) lightnings, thunderings, voices
   _____ (c) seven lamps of fire
   _____ (d) sea of glass, like crystal
   _____ (e) four living creatures
   _____ (f) twenty-four elders

   1. representing the seven spirits of God
   2. the area or object in front of the throne
   3. multi-eyed, creature-faced beings (representing all levels of created life); constantly worshiping God
   4. persons of obvious authority, perhaps representative of the Old and New Testament believing community
   5. predominantly green spectrum of color surrounding the throne; a reminder of God's covenant
   6. dramatic sound effects coming from the throne, denoting power and strength

THIRD DAY: Continue in Revelation 4

7. From the study of the meaning of numbers used in Revelation in an earlier lesson, answer the following, as best you can:
   (a) Who or what was represented by the twenty-four elders?

   (b) What did the seven lamps of fire symbolizing the seven Spirits of God denote about God?
   1. His omnipotence   2. His absolute perfection   3. His great mercy

   (c) Whom or what did the four living creatures with their six wings and differing faces probably represent?
   1. all types of earth's living creatures   2. all the rebel angels   3. just themselves

8. Read the following references and underline anything that is similar to the description of God's throne room from Revelation.
   (a) (Genesis 9:16) *"The rainbow shall be in the cloud, and I will look on it to remember the everlasting covenant between God and every living creature of all flesh that is on the earth."*

(b) (1 Kings 22:19) *Then Micaiah said, "Therefore hear the word of the LORD: I saw the LORD sitting on His throne, and all the host of heaven standing by, on His right hand and on His left."*

(c) (Ezekiel 1:26,28) *"And above the firmament over their heads was the likeness of a throne, in appearance like a sapphire stone; on the likeness of the throne was a likeness with the appearance of a man high above it. Like the appearance of a rainbow in a cloud on a rainy day, so was the appearance of the brightness all around it. This was the appearance of the likeness of the glory of the LORD. So when I saw it, I fell on my face, and I heard a voice of One speaking."*

(d) (Isaiah 6:1-3) *"In the year that King Uzziah died, I saw the Lord sitting on a throne, high and lifted up, and the train of His robe filled the temple. Above it stood seraphim; each one had six wings: with two he covered his face, with two he covered his feet, and with two he flew. And one cried to another and said: 'Holy, holy, holy is the LORD of hosts; the whole earth is full of His glory!'"*

9. (a) What songs or hymns do you know based on Revelation 4?

   (b) Why are these appropriate lyrics for hymns or Christian songs?

FOURTH DAY: Read Revelation 5

   10. Write down the phrases from verses 1-5 that indicate the importance and value of the scroll spoken of here.

   11. Who could open it?

   12. Read the following Scriptures and then from the following list write the title or description for Jesus found in Revelation 5 to which it refers.

   the Lion of the tribe of Judah   the Root of David
   Lamb standing, yet as though it had been slain   having seven horns and seven eyes

(a) (Genesis 49:9) *"Judah is a lion's whelp; from the prey, my son, you have gone up. He bows down, he lies down as a lion; and as a lion, who shall rouse him?"*

(b) (Isaiah 11:1) *"There shall come forth a Rod from the stem of Jesse, and a Branch shall grow out of his roots."*

(c) (Isaiah 11:10) *"And in that day there shall be a Root of Jesse, who shall stand as a banner to the people; for the Gentiles shall seek Him, and His resting place shall be glorious."*

(d) (Isaiah 53:7) *"He was oppressed and He was afflicted, yet He opened not His mouth; He was led as a lamb to the slaughter, and as a sheep before its shearers is silent, so He opened not His mouth."*

(e) (John 1:29) *"The next day John saw Jesus coming toward him, and said, 'Behold! The Lamb of God who takes away the sin of the world!'"*

(f) (Hebrews 7:14) *"For it is evident that our Lord arose from Judah, of which tribe Moses spoke nothing concerning priesthood."*

(g) (1 Peter 1:19) *"...but with the precious blood of Christ, as of a lamb without blemish and without spot."*

(h) (Zechariah 4:10) *"For who has despised the day of small things? For these seven rejoice to see the plumb line in the hand of Zerubbabel. They are the eyes of the LORD, which scan to and fro throughout the whole earth."*

(i) (2 Samuel 22:3) *"The God of my strength, in whom I will trust; my shield and the horn of my salvation, my stronghold and my refuge; my Savior, You save me from violence."*

FIFTH DAY: Continue in Revelation 5

13. What happened when the Lamb took the scroll?

14. **Research Question:** Find out what it was about incense that made it an appropriate representation of the *"prayers of the saints"* (verse 8). Use a Bible dictionary or cross reference in your Bible to find this information.

15. From verses 9 and 10, what had the Lamb done for the saints?

16. What phrase describes how far-reaching or how inclusive was the praise for God and the Lamb?

17. How would a scene from your church's worship service compare with this?

Notes

THE THRONE ROOM OF GOD

After These Things....
(Revelation 4:1)

Chapter 4 began with *"After these things...."* John had just finished the letters to the seven churches, which to him corresponded to *"the things which are"* (Revelation 1:19). Here, then, in Chapter 4, was a movement to a new phase of this revelation: *"the things which will take place after this."* He is told to *"behold"* a certain door *"standing open in heaven"* and to respond to a voice *"like a trumpet"* which said, *"Come up here, and I will show you things which must take place after this"* (Revelation 4:1). This may lead the reader to ask the question, "After what?"

Many students of Revelation believe the *"after this"* refers to the time when God's plan for and through the church on earth is finished. They see the trumpet-like voice and the command to *"come up here"* as a parallel of the pattern set in 1 Thessalonians 4:15-17 for the catching away of the church to be with Jesus in heaven. Some other reasons used to back up this view are that (1) the church is not mentioned as being on earth at any time during the description of the seven years of tribulation, but only begins to be mentioned again in Chapter 19 as the wife of Christ, ready for the wedding feast, after the seven years are over. (2) Also, the images, language, and symbols used in Chapters 4 through 18 describing the tribulation period are decidedly Jewish, appropriate since that period has been described as the *"time of Jacob's trouble"* while the *"time of the Gentiles"* has been the era of the church. (3) Finally, in comforting the church at Thessalonica which mistakenly thought it might have missed the return of Christ, Paul told them that the tribulation period marked by the rise to power of the *"man of sin"* would be **preceded** by a time of falling away, evidently from the truth of the gospel. At least in some degree this is already happening: *"For the mystery of lawlessness is already at work; only He who now restrains will do so until He is taken out of the way"* (2 Thessalonians 2:7). Many identify this "restrainer" as the Holy Spirit, and see the catching away of the church, with each of its members indwelt by the Holy Spirit, as a point when

the Antichrist can begin his work almost unchallenged. Those who know Jesus and believe the Scriptures will be gone, and the absence of "salt" and "light" will allow the corruption and destruction of the tribulation period to proceed with speed. Being fully God, the Holy Spirit will not be absent from the world, but the absence of the people who know and obey Him will make a big difference in how quickly Satan's forces come to power.

What John Saw Up There
(Revelation 4:2-11)

On the Throne: In the opening of his gospel, John wrote: *"No one has seen God at any time. The only begotten Son, who is in the bosom of the Father, He has declared Him."* In keeping with this, John does not give a description of God on the throne here that would enable us to see Him with any identifiable human characteristics, but, instead, uses color, light, sound, and imagery to express the incomparable greatness of the vision of that One he was allowed to see. As the vision of the all-powerful Jesus in Revelation 1 prepared us to know better His infinite knowledge of and concern for the churches of Chapters 2 and 3, this description of the throne room of God makes us secure that He is in control and worthy of praise and obedience, no matter how severe the judgment will be that is described in the following chapters.

"He who sat there was like a jasper and a sardius stone in appearance...." These are the first and last stones on the breastplate of the High Priest of Israel, each of the twelve on the breastplate representing a particular tribe of Israel (Exodus 28:15-21). The idea was that the High Priest was to have continually on his own heart, and also present before God, the concerns of Israel. The ancient jasper was like our diamond and the sardius was like our ruby. These, dazzling white, representing purity, coupled with the red of sacrifice, expressed the holiness and yet the compassionate provision for sin that are characteristic of God. John also saw the throne surrounded by a rainbow, *"in appearance like an emerald."* Green, reminding us of the plant life on earth seems an appropriate color to serve as

a covenant symbol surrounding the God of Creation. From heaven's view (in fact, even from an airplane) the rainbow is circular. From down on earth, we only see part of it. The same with God. He sees all, knows all, and continues in excellence, wisdom, and compassion to oversee all things. We can only know partially His great covenant love; the real comprehension of it awaits us in Heaven.

Around the Throne: There is a great debate as to the identity of those sitting on the twenty-four thrones surrounding God's throne. Some say they are angels of a high order with supervisory responsibilities; others counter that angels are not depicted as sitting but serving, and in no other place in Scripture do they wear the gold crown of the "overcomer" or winner of a race. That is the origin of the word for crown here: *stephanos,* the wreath or crown given for a certain victory or accomplishment. The number twenty-four is that governmental number of God (twelve) times the number of witness (two). For some, then, the number twenty-four points to the unity of God's plan for salvation through Messiah in both the Old (twelve tribes of Israel) and New (twelve disciples of Christ) Testaments. Also, David did organize the large numbers of priests in his day into twenty-four "courses" (1 Chronicles 24). So, some have thought that these elders represent the priesthood of all believers. The word *"elders"* was a common one used in the government of the church, but the white robes are worn by both angels and redeemed saints in the Scriptures. This mystery might not be solved until we get to heaven but must not be fretted over too much. God would have made it clearer if we had to know it for sure now.

From the Throne: Hollywood could not compete with this sound and light demonstration! Lightning, thunder, and voices came from the throne of God. All this dramatically emphasizing the power and authority of the mighty God on the throne.

Before the Throne: *"Seven lamps of fire were burning before the throne,"* representing the seven Spirits of God. Each of these are seen to represent a particular aspect of the one Holy Spirit. Isaiah had named some of these aspects in Isaiah 11:2 when he

described the coming Messiah: *"The Spirit of the LORD shall rest upon Him, the Spirit of wisdom and understanding, the Spirit of counsel and might, the Spirit of knowledge and of the fear of the LORD."*

Besides the lamps, there was a *"sea of glass, like crystal."* A sea normally is thought to be turbulent, and the sea was used in Scripture to represent the restless multitudes of all nations. However, the *"sea"* in heaven is like glass—smooth, solid, without wave or change. There could be a relationship in this *"sea of glass"* with a piece of furniture built for the tabernacle and later the temple (1 Kings 7:23). That was a brass *"Sea,"* sometimes called a **laver**, which was actually a gigantic brass bowl where water was kept for the constant needs of the priests who had to prepare the animal sacrifices. Again, the "real" tabernacle in heaven would have no need for the cleansing water and so would be correctly depicted as crystal-like and solidly pure (Hebrews 8:1-5). If, actually, the sea of glass before the throne were only meant to reflect and radiate the glory of God to the rest of heaven, that would be a beautifully useful thing in itself.

The four living creatures were also before the throne, *"each having six wings...full of eyes around and within. And they do not rest day or night, saying: Holy, holy, holy, Lord God Almighty, Who was and is and is to come!"* These seem to be a particularly high order of angels, having some similarities with the **seraphim** described in Isaiah's vision of God's throne room (Isaiah 6). They are constantly worshiping God and are joined by the twenty-four elders who leave their thrones to fall before God and offer their crowns to Him in worship. What a dramatically glorious vision of the constant worship due to Him who *"created all things."*

The Scroll and the Lamb (Revelation 5:1-7)

This chapter begins with *"And..."* and so is a continuation of the scene in heaven from Chapter 4. However, suddenly, the focus changes for John from the scene of worship to something God was holding in His right hand. It was a scroll. The passage emphasized its great importance. First, God held it with the right hand, the side always associated with power, honor, or favor. Next, it was written on the front and back, evidently full of important words. Further, it was sealed, not just once, but seven times. Top secret, valuable, or privileged was the information it contained. But what, exactly? First, it seemed to relate to mankind. A strong angel asked loudly for someone to come forward who was worthy of opening it, but none was found. Note carefully that the angel did not ask, "Who is willing?" Many have been willing to come forward because of a desire for power or adventure or glory: Charlemagne, Constantine, Alexander the Great, Napoleon, and even Hitler were all willing. But the question was, *"Who is worthy?"* None on earth, born in sin, could qualify. John must have sensed a great loss for himself and others if the scroll were not opened. He *"wept much, because no one was found worthy to open and read the scroll, or to look at it,"* but he was quickly comforted by one of the elders.

There was One, after all, found to be worthy—the *"Lion of the tribe of Judah, the Root of David"*—none other than Jesus! (See Genesis 49:9; Hebrews 7:14; Isaiah 11:1.) John turned to see Jesus and described Him as *"in the midst of the throne"*—showing His unity with God the Father— yet appearing like a Lamb, standing, though apparently previously slain. (See Isaiah 53:7 and John 1:29.) The resurrected Savior is meant to be seen here with the seven horns and seven eyes representing His position as God with perfect and complete power (horns) and knowledge (eyes). (See Zechariah 4:10 and 2 Samuel 22:3.) The worthy Lamb took the scroll from the right hand of God.

Worship of the Lamb (Revelation 5:8-14)

Whatever the scroll contained, the mere possession of it by Jesus started an outbreak of praise to Him from heaven and earth. The hosts of heaven sang a *"new song"* about the worthiness of Jesus. They used harps and brought bowls of incense, the perfume of which **embodied** the prayers of the saints, always a sweet fragrance before the throne of God. The song was in specific praise for the work of redemption by His blood which freed people from *"every tribe and tongue"*

to leave their low place and be made *"kings and priests"* to God. Ten thousand times ten thousand continued to praise His worth and were joined by *"every creature which is in heaven and on the earth and under the earth and such as are in the sea."*

But What Was in That Scroll?

Some have guessed that the scroll was the gospel, but the gospel was not a sealed book after its mystery was revealed in the New Testament. Others think it is the list of all those who are saved. However, the most biblically consistent explanation is that this scroll gave to the one who was worthy of opening it, the right to restore human beings to the roles for which they were originally created: to a position as kings (implying rulership and dominion over the earth) and priests (a role in which they would serve to bring the lost to Christ and the broken to know His forgiving and healing grace). (See 1 Peter 2:9.) When Adam and Eve chose their will over God's, they lost their place of **dominion** over the earth which God had given them. Satan became the new *"ruler of this world"* (John 12:31). Since a sinless man lost it, it could only be won back by a sinless man facing Satan and winning it back by paying the penalty required; the penalty was death. No man after Adam was ever born without sin, and even if one were, if a mere human offered his life in payment for the debt, he would not have the ability to rise again and enjoy that for which he had paid, much less help anyone else. So, in God's mind, *"before the foundation of the world,"* He had planned for Jesus—none other than God Himself born on earth at a specific time in a human body— to face Satan, pay the penalty, rise again, and claim for all of mankind what had been lost (Revelation 13:8). The scroll Jesus was worthy to hold was the title deed to earth that He had won when He *"redeemed us to God"* by His blood. That is what started the glorious scene of praise in heaven and earth of Revelation 5! In God's plan, the victory was won and all who would acknowledge their Lamb, would be redeemed and promoted as *"kings and priests."*

The prophet Jeremiah had been told to do something that illustrates this principle. While Jerusalem was besieged by Babylon, with no hope of relief, God told Jeremiah to buy some land from his cousin, having the deed drawn up and carefully witnessed. He was to even preserve permanently a copy of the deed. It seemed a senseless thing to do since the property he bought was already occupied by the enemy and God had promised Judah would be removed from her land for seventy years, but he obeyed. He himself never lived to enjoy that to which he had the deed. All his life it was occupied by the enemy. But sometime in the future, God promised, that enemy would be gone and Israel would return to retake and rebuild their land. Then, that title-deed would still be valid for some member of Jeremiah's family line (Jeremiah 32:9-12). This pictures what Jesus did for us. He defeated and removed Satan from our "land" and the title-deed is restored to the rightful owners of that lost inheritance. God's Word is always to be trusted. He did bring redemption to the world through the slain but standing Lamb of God. He is so worthy to be praised!

VOCABULARY

1. **dominion:** authority over; rulership of
2. **embodied:** gave form to; personified
3. **laver:** a container used for washing; from the root word *lava*, to wash
4. **preceded:** went before or ahead of
5. **seraphim:** angels of a high order, having six wings, who surround God's throne with worship, described in Isaiah 6

Notes

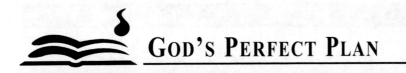

Daily Bible Study Questions

Study Procedure: Read the Scripture references before answering questions. Unless otherwise instructed, use the Bible only in answering questions. Some questions may be more difficult than others but try to answer as many as you can. Pray for God's wisdom and understanding as you study and don't be discouraged if some answers are not obvious at first.

FIRST DAY: Review of Lesson 17

    1. What meant the most to you in last week's lesson?

    2. Was there something new that you learned from last week's lesson that you could share with the group?

    3. To which tribe of Israel did Jesus belong?

    4. What did the incense represent?

    5. How often does the worship of God and the Lamb take place in heaven?

    6. Underline the correct answer: The special seven-sealed scroll was most likely...
       (a) the list of those saved by believing in the Lamb of God.
       (b) the title-deed to the earth previously held by Satan.
       (c) the Ten Commandments.

SECOND DAY: Read Revelation 6:1-6

    7. The First Seal:
       (a) What color was the horse?

       (b) Describe the rider.

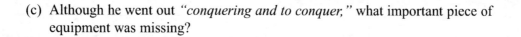

(c) Although he went out *"conquering and to conquer,"* what important piece of equipment was missing?

(d) What are some possible explanations for this?

8. The Second Seal:
   (a) What color was this horse?

   (b) What was the rider granted permission to do?

   (c) What was he given?

   (d) Of what does the color of the horse and the weapon given to the rider make you think?

9. The Third Seal:
   (a) What color was this horse?

   (b) What was the rider holding?

   (c) **Research Question:** Try to find out what kind of price was being asked for a quart of wheat or three quarts of barley. Was it plentiful and being sold cheaply or scarce and being sold for a large amount?

THIRD DAY: Read Revelation 6:7-17
   10. The Fourth Seal:
       (a) What color was the horse?

       (b) What was the name of the rider?

       (c) Who was following behind?

       (d) Over how much of the earth were they given control?

       (e) What would happen to that part of the earth?

   11. The Fifth Seal:
       (a) What did John see when this seal was opened?

(b) What were they asking the Lord?

(c) What were they given?

(d) What were they told?

12. The Sixth Seal: When this seal was opened, an earthquake occurred. What happened...
(a) to the sun?

(b) to the moon?

(c) to the stars?

(d) to the sky and earth?

(e) to the people?

(f) What event would the people think was happening?

13. What is ironic about the phrase *"wrath of the Lamb"* used by those who are terrified by the seal judgments at the end of Revelation 6?

FOURTH DAY: Read Matthew 24:1-42

14. Just a few days before His crucifixion, Jesus Himself commented on these same future events. The disciples asked Jesus two specific and interesting questions right after He described the future destruction of the temple in Jerusalem. Jesus' words had double prophetic meaning—near future (the temple would be destroyed in AD 70, about forty years after Jesus' words in Matthew 24:2) and distant future (it will be rebuilt and

destroyed again near the time of His return). From Matthew 24:1-42 summarize, the best you can, Jesus' answers to these two questions.

(a) *"When will these things be?"*

(b) *"What will be the sign of Your coming, and of the end of the age?"*

15. Compare the verses from Matthew 24:4-11 to the description of the opening of the first five seals in Revelation 6:2-11. Write down the verses which show the similarities you find in the chart below.

	Matthew 24	**Revelation 6**
(a) false christs		
(b) war		
(c) famine		
(d) death		
(e) martyrdom		

16. Matthew 24:8 said, *"All these are the beginning of sorrows."* This literally means "all these are the beginning of birth pangs." Write down what you can find out about birth pangs, as far as intensity and frequency are concerned.

17. How is this information supposed to help us get "ready" for the *"end of the age"* if we can neither know the exact day or hour nor ever remember a time when there weren't wars, earthquakes, famines, martyrs, or inflation somewhere in the world?

FIFTH DAY:

18. Reread Matthew 24:15-31. Jesus speaks here of prophecy again that actually has double fulfillment: first in AD 70 when the Romans invaded but also at the end times when the Antichrist takes over. Describe some specific things about which He warns them that will occur before His return. (We discussed some of these in earlier lessons.)

Note: God does not want us misled about any of His plans, and so He has placed in Scripture, more than once, the details of important events. This can be referred to as a "double witness" and is based on Deuteronomy 19:15. If something you think is important cannot be found more than once in Scripture, be very careful in how you interpret it.

19. Read the following Scriptures, then match them with the verse(s) from Revelation 6 to which they correspond.

   (a) (Isaiah 34:4) *"All the host of heaven shall be dissolved, and the heavens shall be rolled up like a scroll; all their host shall fall down as the leaf falls from the vine, and as fruit falling from a fig tree."*

   (b) (Joel 2:31) *"The sun shall be turned into darkness, and the moon into blood, before the coming of the great and awesome day of the LORD."*

   (c) (Hosea 10:8) *Also the high places of Aven, the sin of Israel, shall be destroyed. The thorn and thistle shall grow on their altars; they shall say to the mountains, "Cover us!" And to the hills, "Fall on us!"*

   (d) (Luke 23:30) *Then they will begin to say to the mountains, "Fall on us!" and to the hills, "Cover us!"*

   (e) (Isaiah 34:5,8) *"For My sword shall be bathed in heaven; indeed it shall come down on Edom, and on the people of My curse, for judgment. For it is the day of the Lord's vengeance, the year of recompense for the cause of Zion."*

   (f) (Joel 3:14-16) *"Multitudes, multitudes in the valley of decision! For the day of the LORD is near in the valley of decision. The sun and moon will grow dark, and the stars will diminish their brightness. The LORD also will roar from Zion, and utter His voice from Jerusalem; the heavens and earth will shake; but the LORD will be a shelter for His people, and the strength of the children of Israel."*

   (g) (Zephaniah 1:14-18) *"The great day of the LORD is near; it is near and hastens quickly. The noise of the day of the LORD is bitter; there the mighty men shall cry out. That day is a day of wrath, a day of trouble and distress, a day of devastation and desolation, a day of darkness and gloominess, a day of clouds and thick darkness, a day of trumpet and alarm against the fortified cities and against the high towers. I will bring distress upon men, and they shall walk like blind men, because they have sinned against the LORD; their blood shall be poured out like dust, and their flesh like refuse. Neither their silver nor their gold shall be able to deliver them in the day of the LORD's wrath; but the whole land shall be devoured by the fire of His jealousy, for He will make speedy riddance of all those who dwell in the land."*

THE LAMB OPENS SIX SEALS

Introduction

If the seven-sealed scroll is the "title deed" to all that was lost in Eden, but won back at Calvary, then the judgments that follow the opening of each seal begin the clearing away of the enemy who has held the earth for so long. This and the other series of judgments set the stage for the reclaiming and renewing of the earth by Jesus on behalf of those whom He has saved. The order of the first four seal judgments is the same as Jesus Himself described in Matthew 24 to His disciples, shortly before His crucifixion, to make them aware of what would happen shortly before His return. However, in Revelation, they are described so vividly that they can be easily committed to memory. The visions describing the first four seals are often referred to as the "four horsemen of the apocalypse." These do not all seem to represent individuals as much as they represent world conditions. The six "seal" judgments are thought by many to occur during the first two years of the the tribulation period. The opening of the seventh "seal" introduces seven trumpet judgments. The sounding of the seventh trumpet introduces the last series of seven—the bowl judgments. Many scholars believe these series to occur one right after another, like sections of a telescope pushing out from one another:

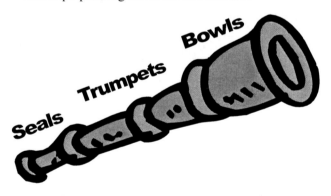

First Seal: White Horse (Revelation 6:1,2)

The color white is most often associated with victory, superiority, or peace. Later in Revelation, Christ is described as coming on a white horse. (See Revelation 19:11.) So, it should not be surprising that one of the common interpretations of the rider

of the white horse is that he is Jesus. He is seen to be riding out first because He is in control of all conquests and ready to supervise all judgment. However, some problems arise with this interpretation. First, the rider has been given a crown, but not that of a king. The rider's crown is a temporary one, like that of a winner of a race or prize, from the Greek word *stephanos*. Whenever Jesus is described as crowned, His crowns are *diadems*, those specifically worn by kings. Further, Jesus' return on the white horse is with much more drama and accompanied by a huge host of angels. He will come to bring ultimate victory for God, and the last two horsemen of famine and death (by disease or mutilation) will not follow His arrival (Revelation 19:11-21). Also, from earlier lessons, we know that a false christ is to appear on the scene, who will imitate Christ, being allowed to have authority for a set amount of time. More like him, this first rider appears on a white horse representing a false peace or victory, and holding only a bow, without arrows.

The absence of arrows has caused some to think that when Antichrist comes on the scene, he may have already used his military strength and so then comes using political or satanic power. Prior to his coming, the attack on Israel by Russia as described in Ezekiel 38 and 39 (or some other country or countries) may occur. This would provide the opportunity for the Antichrist to step forward to act as a peacemaker, offering protection to Israel on the basis of a signed covenant or peace treaty between them. Another view of the absence of arrows or **armaments** to go with the "bow," is that the Antichrist never is given real, long-lasting power that in anyway equals Christ's. The Antichrist is only a temporary king—emphasized by his temporary crown—but who nevertheless operates effectively for a limited time by using deceit and illusion to conquer others.

One thing can be agreed upon, the opening of the first seal ushers in a time of shifting world power, with conquests taking place, most likely through political **negotiations** focused on uniting individual nations by appealing to their own sense of greed and need. That is always the sign of Satan's work—he tempts people to first please themselves, thereby becoming his slaves, while Christ calls men to first deny themselves, serving Him first. Such obedience He blesses eternally.

Second Seal: War (Revelation 6:3,4)

Whenever someone conquers a nation or nations, some will rebel against the loss of freedom or independence. That brings on war. So, following the first seal which brought on a shifting of world power, there came a second horseman on a *"fiery red"* horse. He is permitted to *"take peace from the the earth"* with a *"great sword"* and to encourage war.

Third Seal: Famine (Revelation 6:5,6)

When war is raging, a nation has little time or opportunity to plant or harvest crops. In fact, food production and storage is generally targeted for destruction by the enemy since the absence of food can hurry the surrender of those being attacked. So, very logically, the third horseman rides a black horse and carries *"a pair of scales in his hand."* The scales, along with the words of the four living creatures announcing the price of a quart of wheat, indicate that food will be scarce and expensive. A denarius was the normal day's wage of the common laborer. A quart of wheat was only enough for one meal for one man. Barley was usually considered inferior and used as food for livestock. Certainly since it was a less desirable and nourishing food for people, it took more of it to make a meal. So, the vision shows in both cases that a man working all day would only have enough for himself, with those unable to work, as well as the domesticated animals, being left to starve. Interestingly, nonessentials like wine and oil would still be available.

Fourth Seal: Death Followed by Hades (Revelation 6:7,8)

When the fourth rider was told, *"Come,"* John saw a pale horse with a rider named Death, followed by **Hades**. The word for *"pale"* is really "green," an appropriate color to describe the decaying bodies of the dead. Logically again, war and famine cause physical weakness so that people are left not only vulnerable to disease but also helpless against the

"beasts of the earth." Historical records exist of great plagues following war and famine where people, still alive, were eaten by rats or attacked by birds of prey. Over twenty-five percent of the world's population will die after the opening of this fourth seal. If this were to happen soon, with current population estimates, almost two billion people would die!

Fifth Seal: Martyrs (Revelation 6:9-11)

The scene shifts from earth back to heaven as the fifth seal is opened. The presence of many souls is revealed, those martyred in the tribulation for their faithfulness to the word of God. They cry out to ask God, *"How long, O Lord, holy and true, until You judge and avenge our blood on those who dwell on the earth?"* They are given white robes and told to rest *"a little while longer"* until the full number of martyrs is completed. Here we have an interesting truth revealed to those believing that the rapture will occur before this tribulation period. From the fifth seal, it is shown to be possible to accept Christ during the last seven-year period; however, being a Christian at that time will most likely cost a person his life.

Sixth Seal: Heaven and Earth Convulse (Revelation 6:12-17)

In the Genesis account of Creation, the sun, moon, and stars were said to have been given for signs and seasons (Genesis 1:14). When the sixth seal is opened, these heavenly bodies, visible to the whole world, will undergo frightening changes following a great earthquake. Specifically, then they will be used as "signs" of God's judgment. So frightening will this be for mankind—regardless of wealth, race, or strength—that people will beg to be killed to avoid facing the *"great day of His wrath."*

An Important Question

The last verse of Revelation 6 quotes the frightened population of earth, *"For the great day of His wrath has come, and who is able to stand?"* The answer to that question is a sad one: Without God's help, no one will stand. When Jesus returns by the unmistakable sign of an arrival in the clouds, accompanied by saints and angels, seen by the entire world, like lightning in the sky, only those who have accepted His salvation by faith will be saved from final judgment (Matthew 24:29-31). In the next lesson, we will examine God's plan for preserving those who have a special job to do for Him during the tribulation. For us, this side of the tribulation, however, there already is a plan in place for overcoming the troubles that face us in this present world. Acceptance of Christ's sacrifice, that is, belief in His name and the Bible's claims of what He did for us, will see us through now and forever: *"For whatever is born of God overcomes the world. And this is the victory that has overcome the world; our faith. Who is he who overcomes the world, but he who believes that Jesus is the Son of God?"* (1 John 5:4,5).

VOCABULARY

1. **armaments:** military supplies and weapons
2. **Hades:** the name of the place where the unrighteous dead go until judgment (See Luke 16:23 and Revelation 20:13.)
3. **negotiations:** conferences among people or representatives of groups to achieve agreement

Notes

Notes

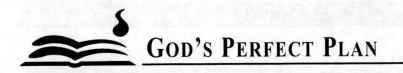

Daily Bible Study Questions

Study Procedure: Read the Scripture references before answering questions. Unless otherwise instructed, use the Bible only in answering questions. Some questions may be more difficult than others but try to answer as many as you can. Pray for God's wisdom and understanding as you study and don't be discouraged if some answers are not obvious at first.

FIRST DAY: Review of Lesson 18

1. From Revelation 6, give the color of each horse and the mission of each rider.
   (a) The First Seal:

   (b) The Second Seal:

   (c) The Third Seal:

   (d) The Fourth Seal:

2. What things not already described above will happen before Christ returns according to Matthew 24?

3. What will be the unmistakable sign of His return given in Matthew 24?

SECOND DAY: Read Revelation 7

4. What were the four angels ready to do in verses 1-3?

5. For what did they have to wait?

6. How many were to be sealed and what did they have in common?

7. Think of what a "seal" is used for even in our day. Write out below what you know about the purposes of a "seal."

8. Read Revelation 14:1. What was at least one purpose for God's sealing of these 144,000?

THIRD DAY: Continue in Revelation 7

9. Who were the white-robed people worshiping God described as coming from all nations?

10. Revelation 7:9 begins with *"After these things...."* What connection do you think there is in the sealing of the 144,000 Jews and the multitude from all nations *"which no one could number"?*

11. What do the *"souls"* under the altar of Revelation 6:9-11 have in common with this *"great multitude"* of Chapter 7?

12. These martyrs of Chapter 7 no longer faced tribulation but, instead, were promised what blessings?

13. Find out what "tribulation" means.

FOURTH DAY: Read Revelation 8

14. What happened at the opening of the seventh seal and what do you think that meant?

15. What can you learn about the importance and effectiveness of the prayers of the saints in these early verses of Chapter 8?

16. Before examining the seven trumpet judgments, read the following verses from the Old Testament and match each one with the correct purpose of that particular trumpet blast for the people of Israel.

    _____ (a) (Joshua 6:5) *"It shall come to pass, when they make a long blast with the ram's horn, and when you hear the sound of the trumpet, that all the people shall shout with a great shout; then the wall of the city will fall down flat. And the people shall go up every man straight before him."*

    _____ (b) (Judges 6:34) *"But the Spirit of the LORD came upon Gideon; then he blew the trumpet, and the Abiezrites gathered behind him."*

    _____ (c) (Nehemiah 4:20) *"Wherever you hear the sound of the trumpet, rally to us there. Our God will fight for us."*

_____ (d) (Psalm 81:3) *"Blow the trumpet at the time of the New Moon, at the full moon, on our solemn feast day."*

_____ (e) (Psalm 150:3) *"Praise Him with the sound of the trumpet; Praise Him with the lute and harp!"*

_____ (f) (Ezekiel 33:5) *"He heard the sound of the trumpet, but did not take warning; his blood shall be upon himself. But he who takes warning will save his life."*

1. as a warning of danger
2. to assemble together for a meeting or announcement
3. to assemble for war
4. to begin battle or carry out God's judgment in a unified manner
5. to call people to worship
6. to praise God in worship

17. Which of the above seemed to be the purpose(s) of the trumpet judgments in Chapter 8?

FIFTH DAY: Continue in Revelation 8

18. Complete the chart below.

	What fell from or happened in the heavens?	**What was the damage?**
(a) First Trumpet		
(b) Second Trumpet		
(c) Third Trumpet		
(d) Fourth Trumpet		

19. Try to describe what life on earth would be like after these judgments. What would people do to or for each other during such a time?

20. To prevent us from thinking the worst was over, what does verse 13 indicate about the future?

21 Read the following passage where Jesus used *"woe"* in His words to His audience from the cities of Chorazin and Bethsaida where He had performed miracles of healing and fed five thousand in the wilderness.

(Luke 10:13,14) *"Woe to you, Chorazin! Woe to you, Bethsaida! For if the mighty works which were done in you had been done in Tyre and Sidon, they would have repented long ago, sitting in sackcloth and ashes. But it will be more tolerable for Tyre and Sidon at the judgment than for you."*

(a) From this passage, and what we have studied so far in Revelation, why does God perform "miracles"—either the kind bringing help or the kind bringing judgment?

(b) Write down an example from your own life about when a "miracle" of mercy or judgment brought you (or should have brought you) to a place of honesty or humility before God.

SEALING, SILENCE, AND SOUNDING OF TRUMPETS

Pause in the Action (Revelation 7:1-8)

After the description of the destructive judgments of the sixth seal, there is a **poignant** pause in the action. John sees four angels, holding back *"the four winds of the earth"* which evidently were about to be used to blow forth further judgments on the world. God ordered the pause so that 144,000 Jews, 12,000 from each of the twelve tribes of Israel, could be sealed on the forehead with the *"seal of the living God."*

In our culture, we use seals to protect the contents of something from contamination or loss; to show origin, proof of inspection, or quality; and even to insure privacy or guarantee secrecy. The Holy Spirit has been given to Christians as a "seal"of their salvation (Ephesians 1:13,14; 4:30; 2 Corinthians 1:21,22). God's seal on these 144,000 was evidently a seal of protection during the great tribulation so that they could witness for Him. When John sees the vision of Christ returning to Mount Zion in Revelation 14:1, these 144,000 with *"His Father's name written on their foreheads"* are with Jesus. They are described as unmarried men, never having had sexual relations with women, *"who follow the Lamb wherever He goes."* They are *"redeemed from among men, being firstfruits to God and to the Lamb"* (Revelation 14:4).

The term *"firstfruits"* is interesting here. The nation of Israel celebrated a special day during the week of Passover in which they offered to God, as a sacrifice, the very first of their spring crop. (See Exodus 23 and Leviticus 23.) Then they went home and made normal use of the rest. *"Firstfruits"* is the first part of a larger harvest. The 144,000 were the first of a much larger harvest of redeemed persons to come out of the great tribulation.

In Matthew 24:14, Jesus had said that prior to *"the end,"* the gospel would be preached to all the world. Many think that these 144,000 Jewish men, redeemed by the blood of Christ, will be the evangelists who will take the gospel to the ends of the earth before Christ's return. Of course, right now in the Church Age, we operate under the Great Commission (Matthew 28:19) which orders us to be about that same task of worldwide evangelism and disciple-making. But, some see the 144,000 as tribulation evangelists of the same quality and zeal as the Apostle Paul after he surrendered his life to Jesus.

Too Many to Count (Revelation 7:9-17)

"After these things"—referring to the sealing of the 144,000 from the 12 tribes of Israel—John looked and saw *"a great multitude which no one could number, of all nations, tribes, peoples, and tongues, standing before the throne and before the Lamb, clothed with white robes, with palm branches in their hands."* The *"after these things"* seems to form a connection between the activities of the sealed 144,000 and the salvation of this innumerable multitude. John was told that these were those who (literally in the Greek) are coming out of the great tribulation. This multitude praises God and the Lamb, as the source of all salvation. The hosts of heaven join in that praise.

These martyrs are brought into the presence of God, robed in white that depicts righteousness, and carrying palm branches, symbolic of peace. Their troubles are over, and they are cared for and comforted by God Himself.

The Seventh Seal: Silence in Heaven (Revelation 8:1)

When the seventh seal was opened, there was an arresting of the normally constant praise around God's throne, and silence came to heaven for *"about half an hour."* Often, silence can be more powerful than continual sound. Silence is often a signal that there is a break in relationship or communication. It can be a pause in preparation for further movement. It can become a moment of mercy if one uses it to stop and assess what has happened, and then moves to repentance so as to avoid further judgment. Perhaps all are indicated here. The silence in heaven was as dramatic and threatening as the eye of a hurricane. All heaven held its breath to await the next judgment of God on an unrepentant world.

Prayers of the Saints (Revelation 8:2-5)

For the second time in Revelation, the prayers of the saints are mentioned. So precious are they, that incense is mingled with them as they are offered on the golden altar. They ascend right up to God—neither lost nor forgotten. Perhaps in answer to those asking God to finish His judgment, the angel takes fire from the same altar and throws it to the earth, causing *"noises, thunderings, lightnings, and an earthquake."*

This short episode should wake us up to the importance of prayer. Time spent in prayer to God is an ever-growing investment, never a waste. Prayer is used to direct the power of God to specific situations. If we would only grab on to that truth and increase our time in prayer and widen the scope of our prayers, we might see more dramatic changes in the situations around us now. As James wrote, *"...you do not have because you do not ask"* (James 4:2).

The Trumpet Judgments (Revelation 8:6-12)

The opening of the seventh seal in Revelation 8:1 prepared the way for the beginning of the trumpet judgments. Four angels *"sounded"* in turn in this chapter, their trumpet blasts resulting in tragic devastation on earth. With some similarities to the plagues on Egypt when Pharaoh refused to let Israel go free, many believe that these are literal catastrophes, even if unusual, that will horrify those living on earth at the time.

First Trumpet: Hail, the normal kind that we often experience, is very damaging to property, vehicles, crops, and animal life. But, here, it is hail mixed with fire and blood, making the damage even more severe. A third of the trees and all the grass is burned by the fire of this judgment. Think of the devastation! Even the air breathed would be affected seriously if one third of the trees were destroyed and fires were burning at the same time in extensive areas.

Second Trumpet: Whether a **meteorite** or **asteroid,** as portrayed in recent movies, *"something like a great mountain burning with fire was thrown into the sea."* The sea turned to blood and one third of the creatures of the sea died while one third of the ships were destroyed. Some huge foreign object falling at great speed in a sea could certainly poison it, but it would also cause huge tidal waves, flooding, and extensive damage to shore lines. This is not a peaceful scene. Which sea is affected? Many believe that the Mediterranean, being the most familiar to John, is meant here. That body of water is very near three continents: Africa, Asia, and Europe. This would be a very effective target for causing maximum damage to huge numbers of people.

Third Trumpet: A great star from heaven, called Wormwood, falls to the earth to poison a third of all fresh water. Many deaths from poisoning result. Wormwood is a native plant of the Middle East described as having a bitter juice, **unpalatable**, and when drunk alone, poisonous (Deuteronomy 29:18; Proverbs 5:4).

Fourth Trumpet: As mentioned in an earlier lesson, God created the sun, moon, and stars for the purpose of marking time and seasons, as well as for His use as signs to get the attention of mankind. The fourth trumpet judgment causes changes in the sun, moon, and stars as a sign of God's wrath. He reduces all their light-giving or reflecting ability by one third. This is a most frightening and damaging phenomenon. This would allow more opportunity for the evil deeds that use darkness as a cover as well as less light for work or growing of crops. Isaiah had warned of this judgment centuries before:

Behold, the day of the LORD comes, cruel, with both wrath and fierce anger, to lay the land desolate; and He will destroy its sinners from it. For the stars of heaven and their constellations will not give their light; the sun will be darkened in its going forth, and the moon will not cause its light to shine. "I will punish the world for its evil, and the wicked for their iniquity; I will halt the arrogance of the proud, and will lay low the haughtiness of the terrible. I will make a mortal more rare than fine gold, a man more than the golden wedge of Ophir. Therefore I will shake the heavens, and the earth will move out of her place, in the wrath of the LORD of hosts and in the day of His fierce anger" (Isaiah 13:9-13).

More to Come (Revelation 8:13)

John then sees and hears an *"angel flying through the midst of heaven"* announcing that the three remaining trumpets are about to sound. How bad will their judgments be? Very bad, indeed: *"Woe, woe, woe, to the inhabitants of the earth."* The worst is yet to come.

How Much Does It Take?

Looking back at the visions John had in this lesson, we must ask ourselves, "How much judgment does it take to get my attention?" To a misbehaving child, a mother asked, "Just how mean do I have to be, before you will behave?" A loving but holy God would have us answer that same question. How long will it take us to see that all the things that are wrong in our lives may very well be the result of our own rebellious lifestyle or a series of unconfessed sins? What will it take to turn us around? For some of us, a pause of merciful relief from a lifetime of problems could cause us to turn to God in overwhelming gratitude and surrender. But, more often, it takes tragedy or disaster to get us to see that we cannot continue without God's help. On this side of the great tribulation, we can still repent and the judgments will be stopped, because of the price Jesus already paid. Today we have the wonderful opportunity to turn from judgment to grace. Will we do it?

VOCABULARY

1. **asteroid:** one of thousands of small rocky celestial bodies found between Jupiter and Mars
2. **meteorite:** a stony or metallic mass of a meteor which reaches the earth after partially burning in the atmosphere
3. **poignant:** memorable; emotionally meaningful
4. **unpalatable:** distasteful; disagreeable to the senses

Notes

Notes

Study Procedure: Read the Scripture references before answering questions. Unless otherwise instructed, use the Bible only in answering questions. Some questions may be more difficult than others but try to answer as many as you can. Pray for God's wisdom and understanding as you study and don't be discouraged if some answers are not obvious at first.

FIRST DAY: Review of Lesson 19

1. What had to be done before the four winds were released to harm the earth and the sea?

2. How many from each tribe of Israel were sealed on their foreheads as servants of God?

3. How many martyrs of the tribulation were present around the throne praising God?

4. Who will lead the martyrs as their shepherd?

5. What happened in heaven when the seventh seal was opened?

6. How many angels were given trumpets?

7. With what were the prayers of the saints mixed?

8. What was the name of the star that fell and polluted a third of the fresh waters?

9. What did the flying angel say after the first four trumpets sounded?

SECOND DAY: Read Revelation 9:1-12

10. What happened when the fifth angel sounded his trumpet?

11. What came out of the bottomless pit?
    (a)
    (b)

12. Though the description was quite strange, fill in the details about these devilish creatures:
   (a) They were not allowed to

   (b) They were allowed to

   (c) The shape was like

   (d) On their heads were

   (e) They had hair like

   (f) Their teeth were like

   (g) They had breastplates like

   (h) Their wings sounded like

   (i) Their tails were like

   (j) Their power was to hurt men for

   (k) Their king was an angel named

THIRD DAY: Read Revelation 9:13-21

13. What was the sixth angel told to do after sounding the trumpet?

14. How many people were to be killed?

15. If the population of the world at the beginning of the tribulation were 8 billion, what would it be at this point? [Don't forget what happened at the fourth seal (Revelation 6:8) and the third trumpet (Revelation 8:11).]

16. Describe the army that was to accomplish this destruction.
   (a) their number

     (b) their colors

     (c) their horses

     (d) their means of killing

17. What was the response of the survivors after the fifth and sixth trumpet judgments?

FOURTH DAY: Continue in Revelation 9

18. **Research Question:** Find out what the Greek word translated "sorceries" in verse 21 is and then comment on how that is appropriate for describing a major problem in our day.

19. What sort of objects of gold, silver, brass, stone, or wood could modern man be guilty of idolizing?

20. How common are the sins of sexual immorality and stealing in our day?

21. Why are the sins listed in verses 20 and 21 so difficult for people to give up?

FIFTH DAY:

22. Centuries ago, following a devastating locust invasion, the prophet Joel warned of an even worse judgment that would precede the day of the Lord. Read the following excerpts from that prophecy and then comment on any similarities you find with the fifth and sixth trumpet judgments of Revelation 9 and any actions that should be taken in preparation for it.

(Joel 2:1-14) *Blow the trumpet in Zion, and sound an alarm in My holy mountain! Let all the inhabitants of the land tremble; for the day of the LORD is coming, for it is at hand: a day of darkness and gloominess, a day of clouds and thick darkness, like the morning clouds spread over the mountains. A people come, great and strong, the like of whom has never been; nor will there ever be any such after them, even for many successive generations. A fire devours before them, and behind them a flame burns; the land is like the Garden of Eden before them, and behind them a desolate wilderness; surely nothing shall escape them. Their appearance is like the appearance of horses; and like swift steeds, so they run. With a noise like chariots over mountaintops they leap, like the noise of a flaming fire that devours the stubble, like a strong people set in battle array. Before them the people writhe in pain; all faces are drained of color. They run like mighty men, they climb the wall like men of war; every one marches in formation, and they do not break ranks. They do not push one another; every one marches in his own column. Though they lunge between the weapons, they are not cut down. They run to and fro in the city, they run on the wall; they climb into the houses, they enter at the windows like a thief. The earth quakes before them, the heavens tremble; the sun and moon grow dark, and the stars diminish their brightness. The LORD gives voice before His army, for His camp is very great; for strong is the One who executes His word. For the day of the LORD is great and very terrible; who can endure it? "Now, therefore," says the LORD, "turn to Me with all your heart, with fasting, with weeping, and with mourning." So rend your heart, and not your garments; return to the LORD your God, for He is gracious and merciful, slow to anger, and of great kindness; and He relents from doing harm. Who knows if He will turn and relent, and leave a blessing behind Him—a grain offering and a drink offering for the LORD your God?*

23. From verses 12-14 of the Joel 2 passage above, what should have been the response of *"the rest of mankind who were not killed by these plagues"*?

24. Write your own question here about something that was not covered or about which you are concerned from these two chapters in Revelation and Joel.

FIFTH AND SIXTH TRUMPET JUDGMENTS

Hard to Imagine: Demon-Locusts (Revelation 9:1-12)

The destruction of the first four trumpet judgments dramatically affected the land, oceans, and rivers, as well as the sun, moon, and stars. Yet, the angel warned of three worse woes to follow. When the fifth angel sounded the trumpet, a star fell from heaven to earth. This star represented an angel who is given the key to open the bottomless pit, a place set aside by God for the confinement of demon spirits or fallen angels (2 Peter 2:4 and Matthew 25:41). It is sometimes called the abyss or Tartarus, the lowest level of Hades which was the waiting place of the wicked dead (Luke 16:20-23).

Out of the opened pit poured smoke and demon-locusts. The smoke, often a sign of judgment, caused the polluted air to block the light of the sun. The creatures that rose up with the smoke were not like common locusts who strip all vegetation as they travel in immense "armies" over an area. These were not allowed to harm *"any green thing."* The judgment of immense pain they delivered was for the "unsealed" human population only; those with God's seal would be spared. Back during the plagues on Egypt, God had caused the same difference to be made between His people Israel and the Egyptians (Exodus 8:22,23).

Evidently, John had never seen anything like these demon-creatures and had to use a wide variety of descriptive elements to describe them. He recorded that they had the shape of war horses, heads with crowns, faces like men, hair like that of women, teeth like a lion, breastplates like iron, and wings as noisy as chariots pulled by running war horses. They could not cause death but could torment a person enough to make him wish for and even attempt his own death. The duration of this judgment was five months. The demon-locusts were under the command of an angel named Abaddon or Apollyon, which translated means "destruction" or "destroyer."

Population Reduction (Revelation 9:13-15)

The suffering of man will go from bad to worse with the sounding of the sixth trumpet. From the golden altar, which earlier had been the scene of the prayers of the saints rising before God, a voice commands the release of *"the four angels who are bound at the great river Euphrates."* The Euphrates River has a long Bible history. It was one of the rivers of Eden; it was given to Abraham as a boundary for his inheritance of the Promised Land; it was at one time a boundary for the holdings of Egypt; and then it was taken over by force as part of the kingdom of Babylon. It will be the scene of one of the bowl judgments later in Revelation.

Bound at the river Euphrates were these angels *"who had been prepared for the hour and day and month and year"* to be released to *"kill a third of mankind."* Since one fourth will have already been destroyed at the fourth seal judgment, the death of one third of that remaining three fourths, leaves less than one half of the world's original population. Less than half, because an indefinite number of people had died at the third trumpet judgment before this. Can you imagine what it would be like if half the people you knew were killed within a three or four year period?

The Army of Executioners (Revelation 9:16-19)

While many prophecy students attempt to identify the nationality of this army, it seems from the context that it is a supernatural army in the same way that the locust creatures of the fifth trumpet are not of this world. The horses carrying these 200,000,000 horsemen seem to hold the killing power. While the riders will wear brilliant-colored breastplates, evidently unconcerned about the necessity of camouflage, the horses will be the real spectacles. They have heads like lions and mouths breathing fatal doses of fire, smoke, and brimstone.

Their tails are like serpents and have the power to also harm mankind.

Survivors Fail to Repent (Revelation 9:20,21)

Defying all manner of good sense, the survivors of the sixth trumpet judgment will not repent of their sinful actions and call on God. They will be deeply involved with the occult—demon worship and idolatry—as well as divorced from any regard for God's plan for moral living. They will prefer to indulge in murder, theft, drug abuse, and sexual immorality. Tragically, these same sins have hold of too many of today's people. We have left the truth of God and have fallen for the lies of Satan. Not even torment or death will wake them up to their need for God. The prophet Joel had written many centuries earlier of attack by such supernatural armies. Through him, God pleaded with His people: *"Now, therefore,"* says the LORD, *"turn to Me with all your heart, with fasting, with weeping, and with mourning."* So rend your heart, and not your garments; return to the LORD your God, for He is gracious and merciful, slow to anger, and of great kindness; and He relents from doing harm. Who knows if He will turn and relent, and leave a blessing behind Him—a grain offering and a drink offering for the LORD your God?* (Joel 2:12-14). Will mankind ever learn?

Notes

Notes